great Kids' cakes

THE AUSTRALIAN
Women's Weekly

CONTENTS

Our aim is to make the job of creating great cakes as easy and fast as possible for the time-poor cake maker. We offer help with any tricky bits by giving you step-by-step photos to follow, and, we use ingredients and decorations that are easy to get in most large supermarkets. Check the last pages of this book for extra tips and know-how. We hope you and the kids have as much fun making — and eating — the cakes as we did.

Pamela Clark

Food Director

Spread tinted butter cream over top and sides of stegosaurus-shaped cake.

Arrange trimmed after-dinner mints along backbone of paper pattern.

Cut mint sticks into graduated lengths and position along back.

Cover body and legs with overlapping spearmint leaves; position cut leaves around neck.

stegosaurus

a delicious mega mint and chocolate dinosaur to set cakelovers' teeth gnashing

for the cake

3 x 340g packets buttercake mix
35cm x 45cm rectangular prepared board (page 108)
1 quantity butter cream (page 109)
green colouring

to decorate, you will need

8 square after-dinner mints
3 x 125g boxes chocolate mint sticks
3 x 200g packets spearmint leaves
Tic Tacs
thin red licorice rope

1 Grease 26cm x 36 cm baking dish (base measurements), line base with baking paper. Using three packets, prepare cake mix according to directions; pour into prepared dish. Bake in moderate oven for about 1 hour. Stand cake in dish 5 minutes; turn onto wire rack to cool.

2 Using paper pattern (see page 108), cut out stegosaurus shape.

3 Place cake on board. Tint butter cream with green colouring; spread top and side of cake with butter cream.

4 Trim all sides of one after-dinner mint; using paper pattern as a guide, position this mint in centre of backbone. Trim and position remaining mints, decreasing in size slightly as they near the head and tail. Cut mints in half diagonally and fit to cake body so that they can be raised along the cut diagonal to look like armour-plated spikes.

5 Cut mint sticks in graduated lengths; place in position along back so that they support spikes, raising each in the centre.

6 Starting at the tail end, cover body and legs with slightly overlapping spearmint leaves. Cut about ten mint leaves in half through the centre, place in position around neck. To decorate face and feet, use Tic Tacs for teeth and claws, red licorice for mouth and a mint stick thinly sliced crossways for eye and nostril.

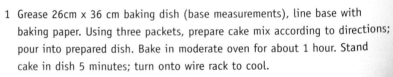

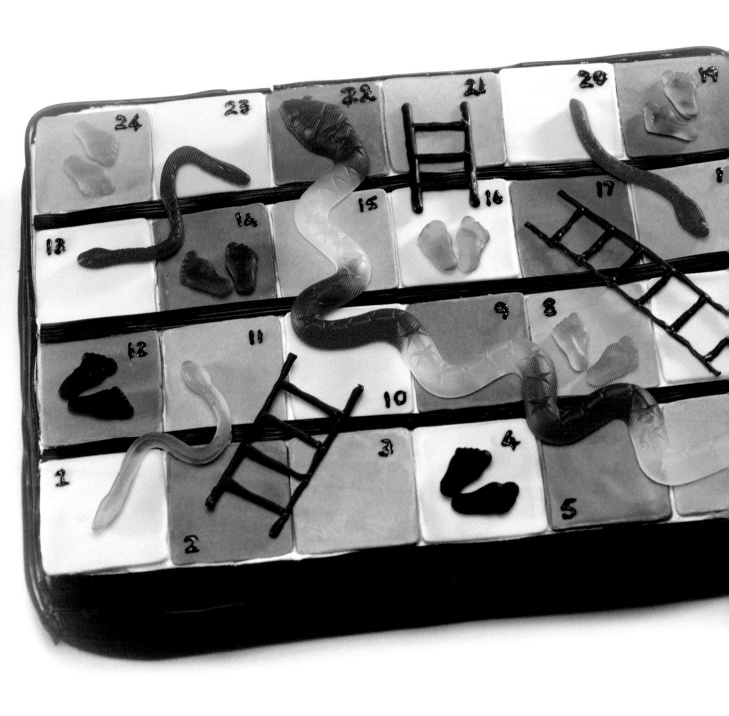

snakes and ladders

children of all ages will be delighted with a cake that makes one of their favourite games good enough to eat

for the cake
3 x 340g packets buttercake mix
35cm x 45cm rectangular prepared board (page 108)
1 quantity butter cream (page 109)
450g white chocolate Melts, melted
royal blue, red and lemon yellow colourings
$^2/_3$ cup (100g) dark chocolate Melts, melted

to decorate, you will need
11 black licorice straps
1 large python snake
small jelly snakes
small "feet" sweets
black decorating gel

1 Grease 26cm x 36cm baking dish (base measurements), line base with baking paper. Using three packets, prepare cake mix according to the directions; pour into prepared dish. Bake in moderate oven about 1 hour. Stand cake in dish 5 minutes; turn onto wire rack to cool.
2 Using a serrated knife, level top of cake, if necessary. Place cake, base-side up, on board. Spread top and side of cake with butter cream.
3 Wrap ten licorice straps around sides of cake.
4 Divide white chocolate Melts among 3 small bowls. Tint one portion with blue colouring, one with red, and one with yellow.
5 Quickly spread each colour onto separate sheets of baking paper in 11cm x 22 cm rectangles. Just before chocolate sets, cut each rectangle into eight x 5.5cm squares.
6 Place alternate colours of chocolate squares on cake, leaving narrow space between each horizontal row. Cut remaining licorice strap into three strips, place licorice strips between each row of chocolate squares.
7 Pipe dark chocolate ladder shapes on baking paper; allow to set.
8 Arrange snakes, "feet" sweets and chocolate ladders on cake. Using black decorating gel, pipe numbers on each square.

Place licorice straps around all sides of the cake.

Measure and cut each colour of tinted chocolate into even-sized squares.

Place thinner licorice strips between rows of coloured squares.

Pipe ladder shapes, using melted chocolate, onto sheets of baking paper.

Spoon each tinted portion of butter cream separately into piping bag.

Pipe lengths of butter cream around edge of cake to form the lion's mane.

Pipe pupils onto M&M's with a little black piping gel.

Paint strands of spaghetti with dark brown colouring.

leonard lion

they'll roar for more of this king of cakes with the triple-treat mane

for the cake

2 x 340g packets buttercake mix
3 quantities butter cream (page 109)
yellow, caramel brown and dark brown colourings
1 tablespoon cocoa powder
35cm round prepared board (page 108)

to decorate, you will need

2 white mint sweets
black decorating gel
2 green M&M's
3 strands spaghetti
1 milk chocolate Melt
1 strawberries & cream sweet

1 Grease deep 25cm round cake pan, line base with baking paper. Using both packets, prepare cake mix according to directions; pour into prepared pan. Bake in moderate oven about 1 hour. Stand cake in pan 5 minutes; turn onto wire rack to cool.

2 Tint butter cream with yellow colouring, divide in half. Divide one half among three small bowls. Tint one portion with caramel brown colouring, the second with caramel and dark brown. Tint remaining portion with dark brown, then stir in sifted cocoa.

3 Using a serrated knife, level top of cake, if necessary. Place cake, base-side up, on board. Spread top and side of cake with yellow butter cream.

4 Position a large fluted tube inside a large piping bag standing upright in a jug. Spoon all the cocoa butter cream inside bag along one side; spoon all the caramel brown butter cream next to cocoa butter cream; spoon all the dark brown butter cream down other side of bag.

5 Pipe lion's mane in swirls around edge of cake.

6 Make eyes by placing mints in position on cake. Using gel, pipe pupils on M&M's and secure to mints with gel.

7 Make whiskers by placing spaghetti on baking paper and painting with dark brown colouring, or you can use wholemeal spaghetti. When spaghetti is dry, break into different whisker lengths.

8 Make nose by cutting milk chocolate Melt to shape and positioning on cake. Make mouth outline with gel, fill in with red part of strawberries & cream sweet. Make freckles on cheeks with gel, place spaghetti whiskers in position.

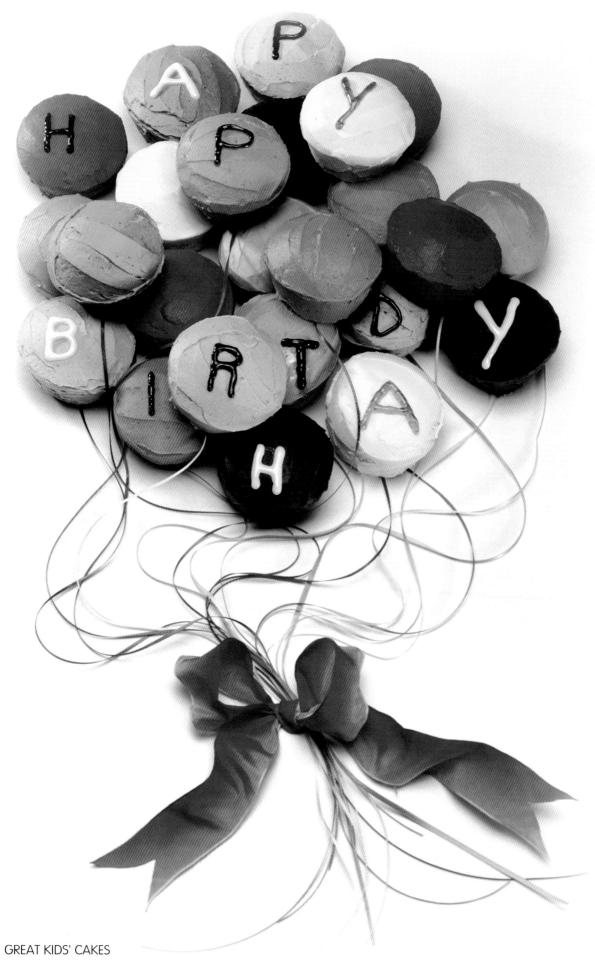

balloon bouquet

**a carnival of cakes to delight your guests –
you could also personalise each cake
with the name of the birthday child**

for the cake
2 x 340g packets buttercake mix
3 quantities butter cream (page 109)
red, pink, green, yellow, orange, blue and purple colourings
40cm square prepared board (page 108)

to decorate, you will need
about sixteen 50cm lengths of narrow coloured ribbons
1m of 4cm ribbon for bow
green, blue, black, red and white decorating gels

1 Grease 2 x 12-hole muffin pans (each hole having ½ cup/80ml capacity).
  Using both packets, prepare cake mix according to directions; divide mixture
  evenly among holes in muffin pans. Bake in moderate oven about 15 minutes.
  Stand in pans 5 minutes; turn onto wire rack to cool.
2 Divide butter cream among seven small bowls. Tint butter cream red, pink,
  green, yellow, orange, blue and purple.
3 Insert a fork into the base of each cake to act as a handle. Spread tops
  and sides of cakes with butter cream. Arrange balloons on board.
4 Using a skewer, tuck ends of thin ribbon under some of the balloons.
  Bring other ends of all the ribbons together to tie with thick ribbon.
  Using decorating gel, pipe a letter on each balloon to spell out the
  appropriate message, if desired.

*Tint each portion of butter cream with
each of the colourings.*

*Using a fork as a handle, spread top
and side of each cake with a different
coloured butter cream.*

*Arrange balloon cakes into a bunch;
tuck ends of thin ribbon under
some balloons.*

Cut out the crown from the cake using pattern as a guide; cut out circles using a cutter.

Place cake circles at each point on the crown.

Form cut lengths of tinsel into circles, twisting ends to hold their shape.

Decorate the base of the crown, below the tinsel, with jube pieces.

crown of hearts
fit for the king or queen of the day, this cake sparkles with edible jewels

for the cake

3 x 340g packets buttercake mix
35cm x 45cm rectangular prepared board (page 108)
2 quantities butter cream (page 109)
pink colouring

to decorate, you will need

silver tinsel
about 35 coloured soft jubes
about 50 love hearts
10cm x 30cm piece silver cardboard
2 x 13g packets silver cachous

1 Grease 26cm x 36cm baking dish (base measurements), line base with
   baking paper. Using three packets, prepare cake mix according to directions;
   pour into prepared dish. Bake in moderate oven about 1 hour. Stand cake
   in dish 5 minutes; turn onto wire rack to cool.

2 Using paper pattern (see page 108), cut crown. Using a 4.5cm cutter,
   cut four circles out of extra cake. Place cake on board.

3 Position cake circles at each point of the crown.

4 Tint butter cream with pink colouring. Spread crown with butter cream.

5 Cut tinsel into four 20cm lengths and form into circles, twisting ends
   together to hold shape.

6 Using scissors, cut jubes into small pieces. Position a length of tinsel on
   crown; decorate with jubes.

7 Position tinsel circles; decorate cake with jubes and love hearts. Cut hearts
   from cardboard, position on cake, surround with silver cachous.

dreamtime lizard

inspired by Aboriginal legend, this striking
cake is distinctively an Australian original

for the cake
3 x 340g packets buttercake mix
35cm x 70cm rectangular prepared board (page 108)
2 quantities butter cream (page 109)
green colouring

to decorate, you will need
1 x 25g packet each brown, purple, yellow, pink,
  orange and blue coloured sprinkles

1 Grease two 20cm x 30cm lamington pans, line the bases with baking paper. Using three packets, prepare cake mix according to directions; divide between prepared pans. Bake in moderate oven about 40 minutes. Stand cakes in pans 5 minutes; turn onto wire racks to cool.

2 Place cakes side by side. Using paper pattern, cut out lizard. Place cakes on board, joining tail and body pieces with a little of the butter cream.

3 Tint butter cream with green colouring. Spread lizard all over with butter cream.

4 Sprinkle edge of lizard with brown sprinkles, then sketch in lizard's markings with a skewer.

5 Sprinkle a row of purple sprinkles around the markings. Use remaining sprinkles to decorate lizard.

Cut out lizard body and tail using the pattern as a guide.

Spread tinted butter cream over top and sides of lizard.

Sketch lizard markings into butter cream using a skewer.

Fill all the markings with different coloured sprinkles.

Use a cutter (or egg-ring, or empty can) to cut completely through the centre of both cakes.

Cut holes from the cakes to make the eyes, a nose and a mouth.

Place strips of green Fruity Metres onto pumpkin and lid.

Roll green Fruity Metre tightly to make a pumpkin stem.

halloween treat

with very little trickery, you can turn two cakes baked in pudding bowls into a fabulously friendly halloween pumpkin

for the cake

3 x 340g packets buttercake mix
28cm round prepared board (page 108)
2 quantities butter cream (page 109)
red, orange and caramel colourings

to decorate, you will need

130g tube green Fruity Metres
small torch
1 large python snake
plastic rat
plastic spider

1 Grease two large 2.25-Litre (9-cup) capacity pudding steamers. Using three packets, prepare cake mix according to directions; pour into prepared steamers. Bake in moderate oven about 1 hour. Stand cakes in steamer 5 minutes; turn onto wire racks to cool.

2 Using a cutter or egg-ring as a guide, cut 7cm-diameter cylindrical holes through centres of both cakes from top to base. Alternatively, remove both ends of an empty can so there is a clean, sharp edge, and use the can as a cutter to remove cylinders of cake from each cake's centre.

3 Cut one of the centre pieces in half; reserve top half for pumpkin lid.

4 Join cakes together with a little butter cream, position on board. Cut out holes for eyes, nose and mouth.

5 Tint ½ cup butter cream with red colouring. Tint remaining butter cream in deep "pumpkin" orange using orange and caramel colourings.

6 Spread cake and lid with orange butter cream. Spread inside and outer edges of mouth, eye, and nose openings with red butter cream.

7 Cut some Fruity Metres into thin strips and place on cake and lid.

8 Roll about 50cm of Fruity Metres tightly to make stem; place on top of the lid. Just before serving, turn the torch on and secure it in centre of cake with a little butter cream. Position lid on top of cake. Decorate cake with the snake, rat and spider.

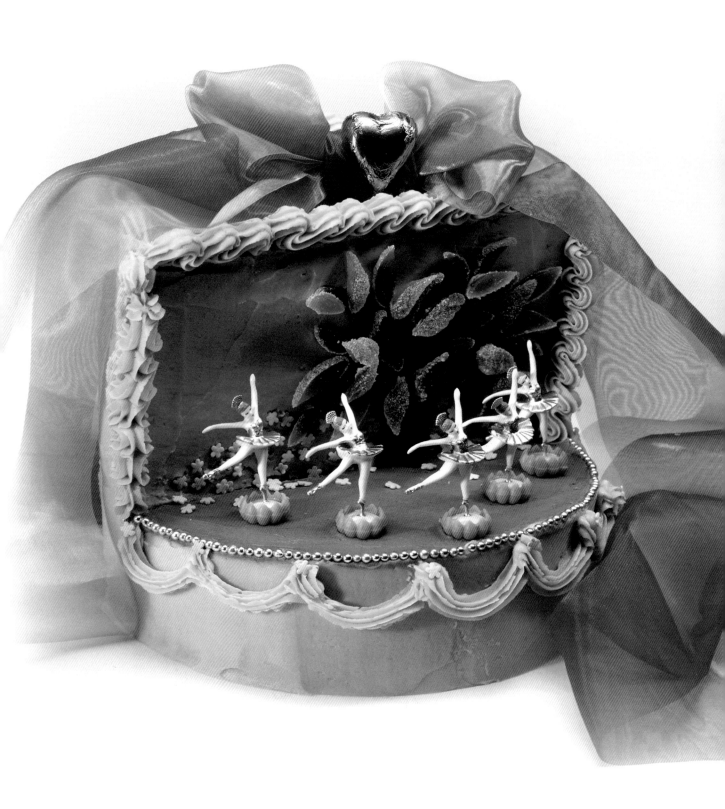

ballerinas on stage

a ballet spectacular that will leave any
prima ballerina stagestruck

for the cake

3 x 340g packets buttercake mix
3 quantities butter cream (page 109)
pink, sky blue and violet colourings
35cm round prepared board (page 108)

to decorate, you will need

about 15 spearmint leaves
6 chocolate mint or coffee sticks
15g packet gold cachous
coloured snowflakes
1 toothpick
1 gold-wrapped chocolate heart
1.5cm each wide pink and pale pink organza ribbon
5 plastic ballerinas

1 Grease two deep 22cm round cake pans, line the bases with baking paper. Using three packets, prepare cake mix according to directions; pour into prepared pans. Bake in moderate oven about 1 hour. Stand cakes in pans 5 minutes; turn onto wire racks to cool.

2 Tint half the butter cream with pink colouring in a medium bowl. Place one-third of remaining butter cream in bowl, tint with violet colouring. Tint remaining butter cream with sky blue colouring.

3 Using a serrated knife, level the tops of the cakes, if necessary. Cut one cake in half.

4 Position cakes on board as shown, securing together with some pink butter cream. Spread top and side of cake with coloured butter creams. Spread stage floor with violet and backdrop with some of the blue butter cream, reserving about half the blue butter cream.

5 Cut spearmint leaves in half through the centre, then cut each half into smaller leaves. Cut mint sticks in half lengthways then into various length for three branches.

6 To make tree, press mint sticks and leaves gently onto backdrop.

7 Using tweezers, place cachous around front edge of stage. Spoon reserved blue butter cream into a piping bag fitted with a small fluted tube. Pipe around stage and backdrop. Sprinkle stage with snowflakes.

8 Insert toothpick into base of the chocolate heart. Tie ribbon into a bow, drape ribbon over top and sides of stage, securing bow with chocolate heart. Place ballerinas on stage.

Spread blue butter cream on side of cakes to make backdrop.

Cut spearmint leaves in half, then cut mint sticks in half lengthways.

Press mint sticks and spearmint leaves against backdrop to create a tree.

Pipe blue butter cream around side of stage in a scalloped pattern.

Place a star-shaped cutter in position on the rocket, then cover inside of star with yellow sprinkles.

Mark a circle in the butter cream, then place a row of M&M's around the circle.

Cut stars from leftover cake using different sized star-shaped cutters.

Spread blue butter cream over tops of star-shaped cakes, then sprinkle with sugar crystals.

rockin' rocketship

blast off! sparks will fly when you launch this rocket

for the cake
3 x 340g packets buttercake mix
35cm x 45cm rectangular prepared board (page 108)
2 quantities butter cream (page 109)
blue, green and red colourings
¼ cup (60ml) apricot jam, warmed, sieved

to decorate, you will need
about 50 blue M&M's
4 thin red licorice ropes
1 teaspoon yellow sprinkles
¼ cup (60g) blue sugar crystals
3 sparklers

1 Grease 26cm x 36cm baking dish (base measurements), line base with baking paper. Using three packets, prepare cake mix according to directions; pour into prepared dish. Bake in moderate oven about 1 hour. Stand cake in dish for 5 minutes; turn onto wire rack to cool.

2 Using paper pattern (see page 108), cut out rocketship; reserve leftover cake. Place cake on prepared board.

3 Tint ¼ cup of the butter cream with blue colouring. Divide remaining butter cream in half. Tint one half with green colouring and the other with red.

4 Following pattern, spread rocket with red and green butter cream.

5 Use red licorice to define and decorate red area, as shown. Place a 5cm star cutter on cake, cover area inside cutter with yellow sprinkles, carefully remove cutter.

6 Mark an 8cm circle on cake, press M&M's upright around circle, then fill the circle with more rows of upright M&M's.

7 Cut stars from reserved cake, spread tops of stars with blue butter cream, spread sides with warm jam.

8 Sprinkle tops and sides of stars with blue crystals. Position around rocket. Position sparklers in cake, light just before serving.

sunflower power
watch their eyes light up for this happy,
smiling flower

for the cake

2 x 340g packets buttercake mix
500g packet ready-made soft icing
icing sugar
lemon yellow, golden yellow and red colourings
1 quantity butter cream (page 109)
35cm round prepared board (page 108)

to decorate, you will need

45g Wagon Wheel
¼ teaspoon yellow sugar crystals
1.5cm x 4cm green ribbon
1 chocolate bee
10cm thin wire

1 Grease deep 25cm round cake pan, line base with baking paper. Using
   both packets, prepare cake mix according to directions; pour into prepared
   pan. Bake in moderate oven about 1 hour. Stand cake in pan 5 minutes;
   turn onto wire rack to cool.
2 On a surface dusted with icing sugar, knead icing until smooth and pliable.
   Tint icing with lemon and golden yellow colourings; knead until both
   colouring are evenly distributed through icing.
3 Roll icing out evenly to about 2cm thick. Using petal patterns below,
   cut out about 25 small, 25 medium and 25 large petal shapes.
4 Drape ends of petals over wooden spoon handles and allow to dry.
5 Tint butter cream with golden yellow and little red colouring. Using a
   serrated knife, level top of cake. Place cake, base-side up, on board.
   Spread cake with butter cream.
6 Leave enough space for Wagon Wheel in centre of the cake. Press petals
   gently into butter cream, using large petals for outer row, then a row of
   medium petals, then a row of small petals.
7 Place Wagon Wheel in centre of cake; sprinkle with yellow sugar crystals.
   Secure ribbon around cake. Insert wire into bee and position on cake.

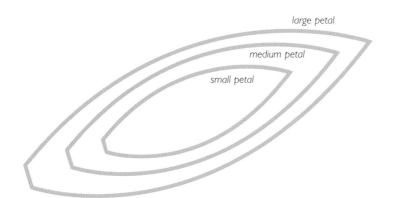

large petal

medium petal

small petal

*Cut petal shapes from icing using
small, medium and large paper
petal patterns as a guide.*

*Place the ends of each petal over
the handle of wooden spoons
and leave to dry.*

*Place a row of large petals around the
outside edge of cake, followed by a
row of medium petals, then small.*

*Sprinkle the Wagon Wheel with
yellow-coloured sugar crystals.*

Cut the face shape from the cake using the pattern as a guide.

Place a long thin strip of licorice around the mouth.

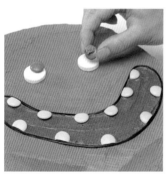

Spoon a little butter cream on the blue Smarties, then secure to the mints to make the eyes.

Position differing lengths of licorice strips under eyes and on rest of face using tweezers.

crazy merv

kids love funny faces so merv is bound to create peals of merriment

for the cake

2 x 340g packets buttercake mix
35cm round prepared board (page 108)
1 quantity butter cream (page 109)
violet and orange colourings

to decorate, you will need

1 black licorice strap
11 green Smarties
2 white mint sweets
2 blue Smarties
about 150g sour jelly worms

1 Grease deep 25cm round cake pan, line base with baking paper. Using both packets, prepare cake mix according to directions; pour into prepared pan. Bake in moderate oven about 1 hour. Stand cake in pan 5 minutes; turn onto wire rack to cool.

2 Using paper pattern (see page 108), cut out face. Place cake on board.

3 Tint three-quarters of the butter cream with orange colouring; then tint remainder with violet colouring. Following pattern, spread cake with orange and violet butter cream.

4 Cut licorice strap into thin strips, position licorice strips for mouth as shown. Cut a small piece off each green smartie and position the larger pieces for teeth.

5 Place mints in position for eyes. Secure blue smarties onto mints with butter cream.

6 Position remaining licorice as shown. Insert jelly worms into top of head for hair.

the big top

**when the kids get inside this tent,
they're in for a big surprise**

for the cake
3 x 340g packets buttercake mix
30cm round prepared board (page 108)
1 quantity butter cream (page 109)

to decorate, you will need
mixed lollies
red, yellow and green Fruity Metres
red shoestring licorice
four 6cm candy canes
1 toothpick
1 cup (90g) toasted desiccated coconut
clown candles

1 Grease deep 20cm round and deep 22cm round cake pans. Using three packets, prepare cake mix according to directions; fill 20cm pan to 2cm below rim of pan. Pour remaining mixture into 22cm pan. Bake both cakes in moderate oven about 1 hour. Stand cakes in pans 5 minutes; turn onto wire racks to cool.

2 Using serrated knife, level top of smaller cake, mark a circle on top about 2cm from edge. Cut out circle and remove centre; reserve centre piece. Place cake ring on board.

3 Place reserved centre piece on top of larger cake. Shape the whole cake into a cone resembling the roof of a tent top. Secure with a little butter cream.

4 Spread butter cream over outside of smaller cake and over tent roof, reserving about 1 tablespoon of butter cream. Fill centre of smaller cake with lollies.

5 Measure heights of side of tent, cut enough pieces of red and green Fruity Metres to this length to position around side of tent. Measure roof and cut red and green Fruity Metres to fit; position on roof.

6 Cut a 70cm strip Fruity Metres and cut 1 edge into scallops. Brush with a little water and attach to edge of roof. Place roof in position. Fold two rolls of yellow fruity meters in half lengthways, twist to form a coil; brush with water. Wrap around edge of roof and base of tent. Secure two ends at front to form curtains. Position red licorice ropes and candy cane tent pegs with a little of the reserved butter cream. Attach a flag made from pieces of Fruity Metres on a toothpick; sprinkle ground with coconut and position clowns.

Sandwich reserved centre piece of cake with large cake; shape into a cone to make the roof top.

Fill smaller cake with lollies, then spread butter cream over cone-shaped cake.

Position lengths of red and green Fruity Metres, alternating colours, around side of tent and on roof.

Place decorated roof in position on top of decorated tent.

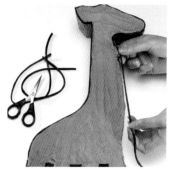

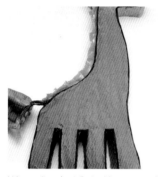

Cut licorice straps into thin strips; then position the strips around the edge of the cake.

Wrap a length of Fruity Metre around a piece of licorice strap; secure tail to giraffe with a toothpick.

Use licorice strips for ear and mouth, jelly bean for nose and bullet for eye; position cut licorice strap for eyelashes.

Cut even-sized diamond shapes from melted chocolate when almost set.

geraldine giraffe

this cake would be the perfect choice for a zoo theme party

for the cake

3 x 340g packets buttercake mix
35cm x 50cm rectangular prepared board (page 108)
1½ quantities butter cream (page 109)
red and buttercup yellow colouring

to decorate, you will need

2 black licorice straps
fruit tango Fruity Metres: 3 x 27cm strips, 1 x 20cm strip
toothpick
6cm piece licorice twists
1 black jelly bean
1 chocolate bullet
²/₃ cup (100g) milk chocolate Melts, melted

1 Grease 26cm x 36cm baking dish (base measurements), line base with baking paper. Using three packets, prepare cake mix according to directions; pour into prepared dish. Bake in moderate oven about 1 hour. Stand cake in dish for 6 minutes; turn onto wire rack to cool.

2 Using paper pattern (see page 108), cut out the body and head of the giraffe. Place cake on prepared board.

3 Tint butter cream brown with red and buttercup yellow colourings. Join head and body of giraffe with a little butter cream, spread cake with remaining butter cream. Cut one licorice strap into thin strips; position licorice around cake.

4 Stick the three lengths of Fruity Metres together to make one thick length; cut into long thin strips but not all the way through the base; position on giraffe for mane. Cut a 1cm x 8cm piece of licorice strap. Wrap 20cm fruity metre around licorice to cover tail; cut end of fruity metre to fray end. Secure tail with a toothpick.

5 Cut some of the remaining licorice strap into thin strips, position on cake for ear and mouth. Cut licorice twists in half, position for horns. Cut jelly bean in half lengthways, position for nose. Cut chocolate bullet in half, position for eye. Cut a 1cm x 2cm piece of licorice strap into thin strips – do not cut through base – position for eyelash.

6 Cover oven tray with baking paper, spread melted chocolate evenly to make a 20cm square. When chocolate is almost set, cut into 2.5cm diamond shapes. When chocolate is completely set, gently lift diamonds off paper, position on giraffe as shown.

starstruck

take the kids on a space odyssey to the beautiful planet saturn

for the cake
3 x 340g packets buttercake mix
1¼ cups (185g) white chocolate Melts, melted
2 teaspoons vegetable oil
yellow, green, blue and pink sugar crystals
45cm round prepared board (page 108)
1 cup (150g) white chocolate Melts, melted, extra
1½ quantities butter cream (page 109)
purple and pink colourings

to decorate, you will need
yellow, green, blue and pink sugar crystals
white chocolate Melts

1 Grease deep 20cm round and deep 22 cm round cake pans, line base with baking paper. Using three packets, prepare cake mix according to directions; pour into prepared pans. Bake both cakes in moderate oven about 1 hour. Stand cakes in pans 5 minutes; turn onto wire racks to cool.

2 Combine melted chocolate and oil in small bowl. Spread chocolate onto baking paper until about 2mm thick, leave until almost set. Using a 5cm round cutter and a 7cm star cutter, cut chocolate into 3 rounds and 17 stars. It may be necessary to remelt and respread leftover chocolate to obtain all 17 stars.

3 Place stars and rounds on oven trays covered with baking paper. Sprinkle shapes generously with sugar crystals. To make sure the crystals stick to the chocolate, heat the shapes in moderate oven for 2 minutes or until chocolate melts slightly but still retains its shape. Remove from oven, leave to set.

4 Trace two saturn rings on baking paper, outline by piping with extra chocolate, fill rings with chocolate. If chocolate begins to set too quickly, place rings in moderate oven about 2 minutes or until chocolate melts slightly, but still retains its shape. Remove from oven, leave to set.

5 Tint half the butter cream with pink colouring, tint the remainder with purple colouring. Reserve about ¼ cup purple butter cream. Place large cake on board. Spoon the pink and purple butter cream onto cake, gently swirl over cake for a marbled effect. Sprinkle with pink sugar crystals.

6 Using a serrated knife, level top of small cake to make it 4cm thick; discard leftover top of cake. Using a 3cm round cutter, cut 16 rounds from remaining cake. Level tops of rounds so they are about 4cm high.

7 Cut four of the cake rounds in half. Use reserved butter cream to secure cake rounds to board around cake, and to secure chocolate stars and circles on cake rounds. Position chocolate saturn rings on cake.

Generously sprinkle chocolate shapes with coloured sugar crystals on baking-paper-lined oven trays.

Pipe outline for saturn rings on baking-paper-lined tray with melted chocolate then fill between the lines.

Cut out rounds all over middle of cake with a 3cm round cutter.

Place a little butter cream on the cake rounds, then secure chocolate stars and circles on top.

Using the small cake as a guide, cut one of the large cakes into a ring.

Using a small sharp knife, cut the cake ring in half horizontally.

Cut one-third of the way through the side of the large cake; discard the ring-shaped piece of cake.

Stack the two small cakes inside the ring on a cake board, then position the large piece of cake on top as the rim.

blooming beauty

nifty cake cutting makes the pot, and silk
flowers top this pretty posy

for the cake

3 x 340g packets buttercake mix
2 quantities butter cream (page 109)
red, yellow and caramel brown colourings
35cm round prepared board (page 108)

to decorate, you will need

chocolate thins
silk flowers
silk butterflies
1 metre ribbon for bow

1 Grease two deep 22cm round cake pans and one deep 20cm round cake pan, line bases with baking paper. Using three packets, prepare cake mix according to directions; divide mixture evenly among prepared pans. Bake cakes in moderate oven about 35 minutes for the 20cm cake and about 45 minutes for the 22cm cakes. Stand cakes in pan 5 minutes; turn onto wire racks to cool.
2 Tint butter cream brown, using red, yellow and caramel brown colourings.
3 Place the small cake on top of one of the large cakes. Using a sharp knife and the small cake as a guide, cut large cake into a ring.
4 Cut ring in half horizontally; reserve one half, discard the other.
5 Place the small cake on remaining large cake, cut a circle 2cm deep, using the small cake as a guide.
6 Remove small cake. Cut through the side of the large cake to about a third of the way down, remove and discard the ring-shaped piece of cake.
7 Place the reserved ring of cake on board. Place the 2 small cakes inside the ring, top with the large piece of cake to form a rim.
8 Trim the edge of the large cake on a slight angle.
9 Spread cake with butter cream. Sprinkle chocolate thins in centre of cake for the soil. Position flowers and butterflies, and tie ribbon in a bow.

graffiti unlimited

personalise the messages scrawled all over this clever cake, which looks just like an inner-city wall

for the cake
2 x 340g packets buttercake mix
25cm x 35cm rectangular prepared board (page 108)
1 quantity chocolate butter cream (page 109)
brown, black and green colourings

to decorate, you will need
1 matchbox
1 tablespoon icing sugar
1 tablespoon drinking chocolate
2 x 30g bars chocolate Flake
¼ cup (35g) milk chocolate Melts, melted
2 chocolate mint sticks
¼ cup (35g) white chocolate Melts, melted
yellow decorating icing
white decoration gel
⅓ cup (35g) desiccated coconut
5 boiled sweets

Press the open end of a matchbox, dipped in combined icing sugar and cocoa, into butter cream to form bricks.

Make telegraph pole by joining half a Flake to a whole Flake with chocolate; secure mint sticks on top with chocolate.

Pipe mouse shapes onto a sheet of baking paper using tinted chocolate.

Make a paint splash on the wall with decorating icing and pipe graffiti messages with decorating gel.

1 Grease deep 23cm square cake pan, line base with baking paper. Using two packets, prepare cake mix according to directions; pour into prepared pan. Bake in moderate oven about 1 hour. Stand cake in pan 5 minutes; turn onto wire rack to cool.

2 Using a serrated knife, cut a 3cm slice form one side of cake. Tint butter cream with brown colouring.

3 Spread cut side of large cake with butter cream; place cake, butter cream side down, on board. Spread butter cream along one end of remaining cake slice; place cake directly in front of large cake.

4 Cut chunks out of top of cake at random. Spread cake and board with butter cream.

5 Wrap matchbox cover with foil, leaving ends open. Dip one end of matchbox in combined icing sugar and drinking chocolate, press gently into butter cream to form brickwork pattern.

6 To make telegraph pole, place one flake on a piece of baking paper, cut remaining flake in half. Secure half of flake on one end of whole flake with a little milk chocolate. Secure mint stick to flake with a little more chocolate. Leave to dry before attaching to board with a little more chocolate.

7 To make the mice, tint white chocolate grey with black colouring. Pipe mice shapes onto piece of baking paper, leave to set.

8 Using yellow decorating icing, pipe a "paint splash" on wall. Pipe graffiti on remaining wall with white decorating gel. Tint coconut with white colouring, sprinkle coconut around base of cake. Spread crushed boiled sweets over board to resemble broken glass. Arrange mice and toys of your choice around wall.

Cover cake with butter cream, using colours in appropriate areas as shown.

Cut thin strips, not all the way through, into a short length of licorice strap for eyelash.

Fan licorice piece and position above the eye in a slight curve.

Position thin strips of licorice on the penguin to outline the stomach, wings, beak and feet.

peggy penguin

a puff of fairy floss makes a soft an cuddly chest for this lovable southern visitor

for the cake

3 x 340g packets buttercake mix
35cm x 45cm rectangular prepared board (page 108)
2 quantities butter cream (page 109)
true blue, yellow and orange colourings

to decorate, you will need

2 slices crystallised orange
1 mint
1 red jelly bean
1 black licorice strap
½ x 30g packet pink fairy floss
50cm x 4cm pink wired ribbon

1 Grease 26cm x 36cm baking dish (base measurements), line base with baking paper. Using three packets, prepare cake mix according to directions; pour into prepared dish. Bake in moderate oven about 1 hour. Stand cake in dish 5 minutes; turn onto wire rack to cool.

2 Using paper pattern (see page 108), cut out the penguin. Place cake on board.

3 Tint half the butter cream with true blue colouring. Divide the remaining half among three small bowls; tint one with yellow colouring, one with orange colouring and leave the third plain.

4 Spread top and sides of cake with coloured butter cream as shown.

5 Remove the rind from crystallised orange slices; using paper pattern, cut pieces to shape of beak. Press gently into position.

6 To make eye, place mint in position, then secure half the red jelly bean to mint with butter cream.

7 To make eyelash, cut licorice strap into a 1.5cm x 3cm rectangle, then cut into thin strips – do not cut all the way through the strap.

8 Fan licorice piece, place in position in a slight curve above the eye.

9 Using scissors, cut remaining licorice strap into several thin strips. Position strips to outline the stomach, wings, beak and feet. Just before serving, press fairy floss on stomach. (Fairy floss starts to dissolve after about an hour.) Tie ribbon into a bow, position on cake.

candy cottage

a gingerbread house that's almost too pretty to eat, but try telling the kids that!

for the cottage
375g butter, chopped
1½ cups (300g) firmly packed dark brown sugar
⅓ cup (75g) caster sugar
1 egg
1 egg white
¾ cup (180ml) molasses
1 cup (250ml) chocolate topping
1.2kg (8 cups) plain flour
¾ cup (75g) cocoa powder
1 tablespoon ground cinnamon
2 teaspoons ground ginger
1 teaspoon ground cloves
1½ teaspoons bicarbonate of soda
assorted sweets and licorice
50cm x 60cm rectangular prepared board (page 108)

royal icing
6 egg whites
1.5kg (9½ cups) pure icing sugar, approximately
1 teaspoon lemon juice

1 Beat butter and sugars in large bowl with electric mixer until combined and just beginning to change colour. Add egg, egg white, molasses and topping; beat until smooth. Stir in the sifted dry ingredients with wooden spoon to form a smooth dough. Divide mixture into six portions, roll each portion into a ball; flatten slightly. Wrap each portion in plastic wrap; refrigerate 1 hour.

2 On a lightly floured sheet of baking paper, roll out each portion of dough to 5mm thick. Using paper patterns (see page 108) and a small sharp knife, cut out walls and roof. Place gingerbread pieces on oven trays covered with baking paper. Bake in moderately slow oven about 40 minutes or until firm; cool on trays.

3 To make royal icing, beat egg whites in a large bowl on low speed with an electric mixer until foamy. Gradually beat in sifted icing sugar, about a heaped tablespoonful at a time, until icing is thick and spreadable; stir in lemon juice. Cover icing with plastic wrap, pressing plastic down firmly onto the surface of the icing to prevent it from drying out during use.

4 Working with one gingerbread piece at a time, spread with a generous layer of royal icing. Position sweets and licorice firmly in icing. Stand about an hour for icing to set.

5 Assemble house on board, using icing to hold walls together. Place tumblers inside house, at each corner, to help support walls while icing sets.

6 Attach roof panels to walls with icing. Use tall tumblers under the eaves to support the roof until set. Place a row of sweets or licorice strip along ridge of roof.

7 Spread remaining icing on board, decorate with more sweets and licorice for grass, fence and pathway.

Cut out wall and roof shapes from dough with a small sharp knife, using paper patterns as a guide.

Place tumblers inside assembled house, at each corner, to support the walls while the icing sets.

Position a row of sweets along the ridge of the roof, gently pressing them into the icing.

Decorate cake board with sweets to create grass, a fence and pathway around cottage.

Wrap cord around each piece of wire; you should have five pieces of cord-covered wire in each colour.

Secure a piece of cord-covered wire onto each love heart sweet with a little chocolate; leave to set.

Wrap half of the orange organza ribbon around the cutter to cover it completely.

Bring the ends of the pink wire ribbon and gold-edged orange organza ribbon up through the cutter, from the sides.

heart of hearts

a message of love in a heart-shaped cake bedecked with ribbons and sweets

for the cake

3 x 340g packets buttercake mix
2 quantities butter cream (page 109)
rose petal pink colouring
40cm round prepared board (page 108)

to decorate, you will need

4m each of yellow, orange, pink and purple satin cord
20 x 35cm long thin wire
^{2}/$_3$ cup (100g) white chocolate Melts, melted
10 small love heart sweets, in assorted colours
10 large love heart sweets, in assorted colours
7cm round cutter or an egg ring
4m orange organza ribbon
2m x 5cm pink wire ribbon
2m gold-edged orange organza ribbon
2m each of hot pink and purple organza ribbon

1 Grease 7cm deep x 30.5cm heart cake pan, line base with baking paper. Using three packets, prepared cake mix according to directions; pour into prepared pan. Bake in moderate oven about 1¼ hour. Stand cake in pan 5 minutes; turn onto wire rack to cool.

2 Twist yellow cord around five pieces of wire, cutting and securing cord at end of each piece of wire. Continue wrapping wire with remaining three colours of cord; you will have five pieces of cord-wrapped wire in each of the four cord colours. Reserve remaining cord.

3 Spread a little melted chocolate on the back of each heart, place wire in centre of chocolate, stand until set.

4 Cover cutter or egg ring with half the orange organza ribbon.

5 Tint butter cream with rose petal pink colouring. Place cake on board, spread with butter cream.

6 Position cutter in centre of cake. Wrap pink wire ribbon and gold-edged orange organza ribbon over side and top of cake, bringing them up through the cutter. Arrange remaining orange organza ribbon with the hot pink and purple organza ribbon in centre of cutter. Twist remaining cord into a single plait, wrap around base of cake.

Spread green butter cream on cake for hat, orange butter cream for face and plain butter cream for mouth, as shown.

cat about town

this rakish fellow has a touch of
the scamp about him

for the cake

3 x 340g packets buttercake mix
2 quantities butter cream (page 109)
green and orange colourings
40cm round prepared board (page 108)

Position mint sweets on cake for eyes.

to decorate, you will need

2 x white mint sweets
2 x blue M&M's
red decorating gel
1 black licorice strap
1 crystallised orange slice

1 Grease deep 30cm round cake pan, line base with baking paper. Using three packets, prepared cake mix according to directions; pour into prepared pan. Bake in moderate oven about 1¼ hour. Stand cake in pan 5 minutes; turn onto wire rack to cool.

2 Leave a quarter of the butter cream white. Divide remaining butter cream between two bowls; tint one portion with green colouring and the other with orange.

3 Using paper pattern (see page 108), cut out cat shape; discard scraps. Place cake on board.

4 Following pattern, spread hat with green butter cream. Spread face and ears with orange butter cream. Spread mouth area with white butter cream.

5 For eyes, place mints in position, secure M&M's in centre of mints with butter cream for pupils.

6 Using the red decorating gel, pipe on clumps of hair.

7 Cut licorice into thin strips for whiskers and mouth. Cut crystallised orange for the nose.

Pipe clumps of hair near hat with red decorating gel.

Cut licorice strap into thin strips to create whiskers and mouth.

Spread butter cream all over body and head of spider, building up mounds for eyes and pincers as shown.

Pipe melted chocolate over markings for legs and pincers on baking paper; set. Pipe over legs two more times.

Make a row of smaller eyes across top of head with Choc Bits, then mark centres with red decorating gel.

Position legs into body and pincers into the top of the head.

hairy scary spider
let them sink their teeth into this monster – there's nothing to be scared of really

for the cake
2 x 340g packets buttercake mix
40cm square prepared board (page 108)
2 quantities chocolate butter cream (page 109)
brown colouring
1 cup (70g) shredded coconut

to decorate, you will need
1¹/₃ cups (200g) milk chocolate Melts, melted
2 red Smarties
2 milk chocolate Melts, extra
5 milk Choc Bits
red decorating gel
black decorating gel, optional

1 Grease two deep 20cm round cake pans, line bases with baking paper. Using both packets, prepare cake mix according to directions; divide between prepared pans. Bake in moderate oven about 50 minutes. Stand cakes in pans 5 minutes; turn onto wire racks to cool.
2 Cut a 12cm round out of a piece of baking paper; use to cut out spider's head from one of the cakes.
3 Tint chocolate butter cream with the brown colouring; stir in coconut.
4 Position cakes on board. Spread the spider's head and body with butter cream, building up four mounds for eyes and pincers, as shown.
5 Draw eight legs and two pincers on a piece of baking paper. Pipe over markings with melted chocolate. Once chocolate has set, pipe another layer of chocolate over the legs to make them thicker. Repeat once more; leave to set.
6 To make main eyes, attach Smarties to the two extra Melts with butter cream and position as shown on mounds. Make a row of five smaller eyes with Choc Bits and mark centres with red decorating gel.
7 Position the legs and pincers in butter cream. Draw in web with black decorating gel, if desired.

a different drummer

an easy shape, this cake is sure to hit the right note

for the cake
3 x 340g packets buttercake mix
2 quantities butter cream (page 109)
royal blue and red colouring
35cm round prepared board (page 108)
500g packet ready-made soft icing
icing sugar

to decorate, you will need
200g red licorice Super Ropes
8 white Kool Mints
2 x 12cm red-and-white striped candy canes (or sticks)

1 Grease two deep 20cm round cake pans, line bases with baking paper. Using three packets, prepare cake mix according to directions; divide mixture evenly between prepared pans. Bake in moderate oven about 1 hour. Stand cakes in pans 5 minutes; turn onto wire racks to cool. Using a serrated knife, level tops of cakes.

2 Tint two-thirds if the butter cream with royal blue colouring. Sandwich tops of cake together with a little of the blue butter cream. Place cake on board.

3 Spread top of cake with the white butter cream; spread around side with blue butter cream

4 Wrap rope around base and top edge of drum (you may need to secure rope with toothpicks).

5 Cut remaining rope into eight 14cm lengths; place around side of drum as shown. Place the Kool Mints in position.

6 On surface dusted with icing sugar, knead icing until smooth and pliable. Tint with red colouring. Roll icing into two balls for drumsticks, wrap tightly in plastic wrap and stand about 1 hour or until firm. If using candy canes, snap off crook of neck, leaving 12cm length of stick; insert broken ends into balls. Position drumsticks on top of cake.

Join tops of cakes together with a little of the blue butter cream.

Wrap red licorice rope around top and bottom edge of drum; secure with toothpicks if necessary.

Place cut lengths of rope on the diagonal around the drum then position Kool Mints as shown.

Insert end of broken candy canes into balls of red-tinted icing for drumsticks.

Cut out whale shape from cake using the paper pattern as a guide; reserve leftover cake.

Swirl blue butter cream into the remaining white butter cream to create a marble effect.

Cut out a spout and flipper from the leftover pieces of cake then position on whale.

Sprinkle blue sugar crystals on flipper, body and tail of whale and sprinkle white sugar crystals on the spout.

wally whale

there's no way to save this whale from a sticky end

for the cake
3 x 340g packets buttercake mix
35cm x 45cm rectangular prepared board (page 108)
1 quantity butter cream (page 109)
royal blue colouring

to decorate, you will need
blue and white sugar crystals
1 black licorice strap
1 blue M&M

1 Grease 26cm x 36cm baking dish (base measurements), line base with baking paper. Using three packets, prepare cake mix according to directions; pour into prepared dish. Bake in moderate oven about 1 hour. Stand cake in dish 5 minutes; turn onto wire rack to cool.
2 Use paper pattern (see page 108), cut out whale; reserve leftover cake. Using a toothpick or skewer, mark out belly on cake. Place cake on board.
3 Tint half the butter cream with royal blue colouring.
4 Following pattern, spread belly with 2 tablespoons white butter cream.
5 Swirl blue butter cream into remaining white butter cream gently to create a marbled effect. Carefully spread marbled butter cream over cake.
6 Cut spout and flipper from reserved leftover cake and position on cake; spread with more butter cream.
7 Sprinkle blue sugar crystals on and around the flipper, tail and belly. Sprinkle white sugar crystals on spout. Cut a thin strip of licorice for mouth and place in position. Cut eye from remaining licorice; position on cake. Secure blue M&M on licorice with butter cream.

supercool superstar

this wiseguy's bright grin will bring out
the party animal in everyone

Cut out star shape from cake using
the paper pattern as a guide.

for the cake

4 x 340g packets buttercake mix
40cm square prepared board (page 108)
2 quantities butter cream (page 109)
buttercup yellow, orange and lemon yellow colourings

to decorate, you will need

yellow sugar crystals
1/3 cup (50g) dark chocolate Melts, melted
1/2 cup (75g) white chocolate Melts, melted
brown decorating gel
child's sunglasses

Sprinkle butter cream-covered cake
with yellow sugar crystals.

1 Grease deep 30cm square cake pan, line base with baking paper. Using four packets, prepare cake mix according to directions; pour into prepared pan. Bake in moderate oven about 1¾ hours. Stand cake in pan 5 minutes; turn onto wire rack to cool.

2 Place cake on board. Using paper pattern (see page 108), cut out a star shape, or cut a freeform star to your liking.

3 Divide butter cream into three portions; tint one portion with buttercup yellow, one portion with orange colouring, and one portion with lemon yellow colouring.

4 Combine the three butter creams in a medium bowl and swirl gently to create a marble effect.

5 Spread top and sides of cake with marbled butter cream. Sprinkle star with sugar crystals.

6 Pipe melted dark chocolate outline for mouth onto baking paper; pipe pairs of straight lines with leftover chocolate; leave to set. Pipe melted white chocolate between the dark chocolate outlines for teeth; leave to set.

7 Outline cake with brown decorating gel. Decorate cake with mouth, sunglasses and straight lines.

Pipe white chocolate into dark chocolate
outline of the mouth to create teeth.

Outline the top and bottom edge
of the star-shaped cake with
brown decorating gel.

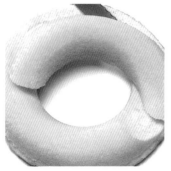

Cut half of one cake in half at an angle without cutting through the base; reserve for the snake's head.

Position butter cream-covered cakes on cake board, with the snake's head peeking through.

Cut even-sized diamond shapes from Roll-ups using kitchen scissors.

Place diamond-shaped Roll-ups along the snake's back, alternating colours.

snaky jim

his sensuous curves are easily achieved with simple savarin pans

for the cake
340g packet buttercake mix
1 quantity butter cream (page 109)
lemon yellow colouring
35cm round prepared board (page 108)

to decorate, you will need
1 packet berry fruits rainbow Roll-ups
black decorating gel
2 green M&M's

1 Grease 22cm savarin pan. Make cake according to directions on packet; divide mixture between prepared pans. Bake in moderate oven about 20 minutes. Stand cake in pans 5 minutes; turn onto wire racks to cool.
2 Using a serrated knife, cut half of one cake in half at an angle, not cutting through base; reserve cake piece for snake's head.
3 Using paper pattern (see page 108), cut out snake's head from reserved cake piece.
4 Tint butter cream with lemon yellow colouring; spread all cake pieces with butter cream.
5 Assemble cake on board, with the various cake pieces topping one another.
6 Using scissors, cut Roll-ups into even-sized diamond shapes.
7 Decorate snake with diamonds, alternating the different colours.
8 Using black decorating gel, make snake-eye slit shapes on M&M's for pupils; position eyes on snake. Place tongue in position. Using piping gel, pipe nostrils and mouth.

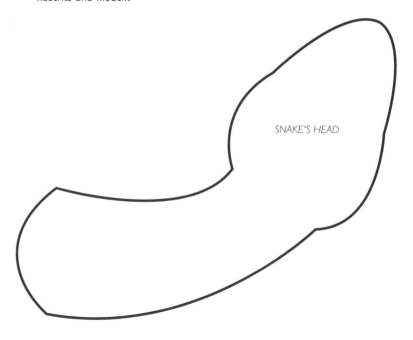

SNAKE'S HEAD

castle of kings
a palace fit for a king

for the cake
40cm x 50cm rectangular prepared board (page 108)
6 x 350g packets chocolate finger lamingtons (6.5cm long)
2 quantities chocolate butter cream (page 109)
2 x 350g packets chocolate lamingtons (6.5cm square)
3 x 280g packets pink lamingtons (7cm round)

to decorate, you will need
4 pink ice-cream wafers
4 wooden skewers
2 cups (300g) dark chocolate Melts, melted
4 ice-cream cones
1 x 20cm long chain
assorted toy soldiers, horses, etc.

1 On board, make rectangular base for castle using four finger lamingtons for the shorter sides and five finger lamingtons for the longer sides; join lamingtons with some of the butter cream. Build a second level on the castle wall in a brickwork pattern, cutting lamingtons to fit. Leave a space on one wall for the doorway. Continue brickwork pattern until five layers high.

2 Cut a wafer the width of a finger lamington for support above door; cut two wafers for castle doors. Position wafer support over door, secure with butter cream on both sides. Build a sixth layer of castle wall with all but two of the remaining finger lamingtons.

3 Position one square of chocolate lamington on each of the four castle corners; secure with butter cream. Cut four square lamingtons in half; position, cut-side down, to form battlements. Cut two finger lamingtons into three pieces each; place one piece in each corner, on top of each of the four square lamingtons. Discard remaining two finger lamingtons pieces and remaining square lamingtons.

4 Stack five pink lamingtons; push a skewer through centre. Repeat with 15 more pink lamingtons. Position one lamington stack at each castle corner.

5 Spread some of the melted chocolate over each ice-cream cone; leave to set. Place a cone on top of each pink lamington stack to form turrets.

6 Trace 6cm x 7cm portcullis shape on baking paper. Pipe melted chocolate over shape; pipe outline around doors and drawbridge. Leave to set.

7 Carefully peel away baking paper from portcullis; position over doorway, secure with butter cream. Secure chain in place with melted chocolate. Position doors and remaining wafer for drawbridge. Arrange toys etc, as desired.

Make the base using four lamington fingers for short sides and five for long sides; join together with butter cream.

Place a square lamington in each corner of the castle wall.

Cover each ice-cream cone with some of the melted chocolate; leave to set.

Pipe a portcullis shape with chocolate on a piece of baking paper; pipe outlines on wafers for doors and the drawbridge.

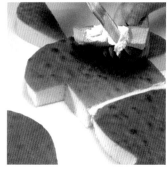

Assemble cake pieces for the mermaid on cake board, joining pieces together with the untinted butter cream.

Tint remaining one-third of the butter cream to a skin colour, adding colour gradually with a skewer.

Spread green butter cream over tail and skin-coloured butter cream over body and head.

Position spearmint leaves over the tail, overlapping and alternating leaves, sugar-side up and cut-side up.

mindy mermaid

with mindy as the star attraction, the party is sure to go swimmingly

for the cake

3 x 340g packets buttercake mix
70cm square prepared board (page 108)
3 quantities butter cream (page 109)
green, red and yellow colourings
vegetable oil, for deep-frying

to decorate, you will need

2 x 200g packets spearmint leaves
3 green musk sticks
2 savoiardi (sponge finger) biscuits
1 red snake
2 strawberries & cream sweets
blue decorating gel
1 black licorice strap
11 sour gummi beans
1 small shell
2 scallop shells
250g bean thread vermicelli

1 Grease three 20cm x 30cm lamington pans, line base with baking paper. Using three packets, prepare cake mix according to directions; divide among prepared pans. Bake in moderate oven about 25 minutes. Stand cakes in pans 5 minutes; turn onto wire racks to cool.
2 Using paper patterns (see page 108), cut out tail and body of mermaid from two of the cakes.
3 Cut out the fin and two semi-circles for head from remaining cake.
4 Join cake pieces on board with some of the untinted butter cream.
5 Tint two-thirds of butter cream with green colouring; tint the remaining third butter cream to a skin tone using red and yellow colourings.
6 Spread green butter cream over top and side of tail and skin-tone butter cream over top and side of body and head.
7 Cut spearmint leaves lengthways through the centre; cover tail with spearmint leaves. Use green musk sticks to separate tail from body. Position biscuits for arms. Cut mouth from red snake. Make the eyes with strawberries & cream sweets and blue gel; make the eyelashes with strips of licorice; make the necklace with gummi beans and small shell. Decorate cake with shells and sweets as shown. Deep-fry vermicelli in hot oil until puffed; drain on absorbent paper. Shape and style vermicelli hair by cutting and separating noodles; position hair around head.

volcano vibes

a mountain of fun in an explosion of
ice-cream, honeycomb and rocky road

Scoop alternate spoonfuls of chocolate,
vanilla and strawberry ice-cream into
the Dolly Varden mould.

for the cake

4 litres neapolitan ice-cream
340g packet buttercake mix
¾ cup (165g) caster sugar
¼ cup (60ml) water
1 cup (90g) desiccated coconut
green colouring
40cm round prepared board (page 108)
600ml thickened cream
¼ cup (25g) cocoa powder
2 tablespoons icing sugar

to decorate, you will need

4 x 375g packets rocky road, chopped roughly
4 x 50g Violet Crumble bars, chopped roughly
½ cup (125ml) thick strawberry topping
5 sparklers

Once toffee has set, peel off the foil
and break toffee into large ieces.

1 Grease a 20cm Dolly Varden mould (2.5-Litre/10-cup capacity), line with
   plastic wrap, extending plastic about 5cm over edge of mould.
2 Separate vanilla, chocolate and strawberry ice-cream into three bowls. Using
   a slotted spoon, push down on ice-cream until just soft. Scoop alternate
   spoonfuls of each colour into prepared mould. Tap mould on bench to settle
   ice-cream; cover with foil and freeze overnight.
3 Grease deep 20cm round cake pan, line base with baking paper. Make cake
   according to directions on packet. Bake in moderate oven about 50 minutes.
   Stand cake in pan 5 minutes; turn onto wire rack to cool.
4 Combine sugar and water in small pan, stir over heat, without boiling, until
   sugar dissolves. Boil mixture, uncovered, without stirring, about 10 minutes
   or until it becomes a caramel colour. Pour hot toffee onto greased foil-lined
   oven tray. Leave to set then carefully peel away foil and break toffee into
   large pieces.

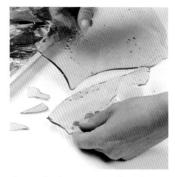

Work the green colouring through
the coconut in a plastic bag until
coconut is evenly tinted.

5 Combine coconut and a few drops of green colouring in a plastic bag; shake
   and press bag until coconut is tinted green.
6 Place cake on board. Beat cream with sifted cocoa and icing sugar in
   medium bowl with electric mixer until firm peaks form. Spread a quarter of
   the cream mixture over top and side of cake.
7 Remove ice-cream from mould, place on cake; spread remaining cream over
   the ice-cream. Decorate with rocky road, violet crumble and toffee pieces.
   Drizzle volcano with topping. Sprinkle green coconut around base of volcano;
   insert sparklers around top of the volcano.

Place moulded ice-cream on top of
cake then completely cover both with
remaining chocolate cream.

Spread chocolate over pattern for chest base and lid, draping the lid over a cylinder shape; leave to set.

Assemble chest by joining two pieces at a time with melted chocolate and supporting sides with tumblers.

Position the chocolate-covered strips of baking paper across the lid.

Outline chocolate bands on lid and sides of the chest with piping gel, then pipe dots for rivets.

treasure chest

pirates are never out of style, and a chocolate chest overflowing with sweets will be treasured

for the chest
340g packet buttercake mix
4 x 375g packets dark chocolate Melts

icing
2 cups (320g) icing sugar
30g butter, softened
1 tablespoon hot water, approximately
35cm x 45cm rectangular prepared board (page 108)

to decorate, you will need
1 x250g packet M&M's
¼ cup (50g) chocolate sprinkles
black and red decorating gel
assorted lollies

1 Line two 12-hole muffin pans (⅓-cup/80ml capacity) with paper patty cases. Make cake according to directions on packet. Spoon mixture into cases. Bake in moderate oven about 15 minutes. Stand cakes in pans 5 minutes; turn onto wire rack to cool.

2 To make icing, place icing sugar in a medium heatproof bowl; stir in butter and enough water to make a stiff paste. Place bowl over pan of simmering water, stir until icing is spreadable. Spread cakes with icing, decorate like pirates' faces with M&M's, chocolate sprinkles and decorating gel.

3 Mark two 20cm x 28cm rectangles on separate sheets of baking paper for the base and lid of the treasure chest. Mark two more 12cm x 28cm rectangles and two more measuring 12cm x 20cm for sides.

4 Melt 500g of the dark chocolate; spread chocolate evenly over base and lid pattern, draping lid sheet over a large cylindrical shape (like a jar on its side). Leave to set then trim edges, reserving any leftover chocolate. Melt another 250g of dark chocolate; spread evenly over the patterns for the two short sides of the chest. Leave to set then trim edges, reserving any leftover chocolate. Melt another 400g of the dark chocolate; spread chocolate evenly over the pattern for the two long sides of the chest. Leave to set, trim edges, reserving any leftover chocolate.

5 To assemble chest on board, melt remaining dark chocolate with reserved scraps of chocolate. Working with two pieces at a time, brush the edges to be joined with chocolate and press together, supporting sides with tumblers until set.

6 Cut strips of baking paper about 2cm wide and long enough to go around the chest's lid and sides twice; spread with remaining melted chocolate. Working quickly, place strips over lid and on sides into position as shown. When chocolate is set, peel away paper.

7 Outline chocolate "bands" on chest with black decorating gel; pipe dots to resemble "rivets" holding bands onto chest. Fill chest with pirate cake and assorted lollies. Place lid in position.

edward bear

it's always a picnic when teddy comes to the party

Cut paw cake pieces in half, then slice at an angle as shown.

for the cake
4 x 340g packets buttercake mix
35cm x 60cm rectangular prepared board (page 108)
3 quantities butter cream (page 109)
brown, red and ivory colourings

to decorate, you will need
1 milk chocolate Melt
2 brown Smarties
2 small red foil-covered chocolate hearts
about 17 red Smarties
75cm thin red licorice rope
35g jar green snowflakes

Cut a rounded shape from top of the remaining cake where the head joins the body.

1. Grease two deep 25cm round cake pans, line bases with baking paper. Using four packets, prepare cake mix according to directions; divide between prepared pans. Bake in moderate oven for about 1 hour. Stand cakes in pans 5 minutes; turn onto wire racks to cool.
2. Using paper pattern (see page 108), cut out bear's face and paws from one cake.
3. Cut paws in half, then slice at an angle as shown.
4. Cut a rounded shape out of remaining cake where head joins body. Position head, body and paws on board.
5. Tint one-third of the butter cream light brown. Divide remaining butter cream into three portions: tint one portion dark brown; another portion red; and remaining portion ivory.

Run a fork through the brown-coloured butter cream for a textured fur look.

6. Using a small sharp knife, mark out trouser line on cake. Spread top and side of cake with butter creams, making nose and belly slightly rounded, and blending in ivory butter cream. Spread paws with butter cream, position on cake. Run a fork through brown butter cream to give a textured effect.
7. Cut one milk chocolate melt into a triangle, place on face for nose. Position brown smarties for eyes. Position chocolate hearts and a red smartie for bow-tie. Make braces from red licorice rope; position smarties in between each pair of licorice rope. Place snowflakes on trousers. Spoon dark brown butter cream into a piping bag fitted with a small plain tube; pipe mouth and front paws. Run a fork gently through butter cream on paws to give a textured effect.

Cut the chocolate Melt into a triangle and position on teddy's face for nose.

Patch any gaps in the top, sides and base of cake with a little icing. Brush top and sides evenly with a little jam.

Lift second layer of rolled-out tinted icing over first layer of jam-covered icing, moulding onto the cake with your hands.

Cut a rectangle from the rolled out reserved white icing for the present's message tag.

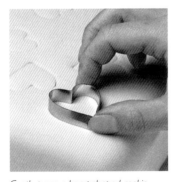

Gently press a heart-shaped cookie cutter into the icing all over the cake.

surprise package
dress up your cake with this pretty gift-wrap idea

for the cake
2 x 340g packets buttercake mix
2 x 500g packets ready-made soft icing
icing sugar
pink colouring
35cm square prepared board (page 108)
½ cup (125ml) apricot jam, warmed, strained

to decorate, you will need
1 non-toxic felt-tip pen
heart-shaped cutter
1m x 5cm purple ribbon
1m x 2.5cm purple ribbon
assorted fresh or silk flowers

1 Grease deep 23cm square cake pan, line base with baking paper. Using two packets, prepare cake mix according to directions; pour into prepared pan. Bake in moderate oven about 1 hour. Stand cake in pan for 5 minutes; turn onto wire rack to cool. Using a serrated knife, level top of cake.

2 On a surface dusted with icing sugar, knead icing until smooth. Reserve 1 tablespoon icing for message tag. Knead colouring into remaining icing.

3 Place cake, base-side up, on board. Patch top, sides and base of cake with a little of the icing. Brush top and sides of cake evenly with some of the jam.

4 Divide pink icing in half tightly in plastic wrap. On a surface dusted with icing sugar, roll out other half of icing until large enough to cover top and sides of cake. Lift icing over cake then mould icing onto cake with hands dusted with icing sugar; trim edges of cake neatly. Brush top and sides of cake with more jam. Repeat process with remaining half of the pink icing.

5 Roll out reserved white icing until about 2mm thick; cut into a 3cm x 8cm rectangle for message tag, decorate as desired; leave to become firm. Using the non-toxic pen, write a birthday message on the tag.

6 Gently press a small heart-shaped cutter into icing all around cake. Position ribbons as for a present, tucking ends under cake. Decorate top of cake with flowers and tag.

skateboard dog

a radical character if ever there was one

for the cake

3 x 340g packets buttercake mix
40cm x 50cm rectangular prepared board (page 108)
2 quantities butter cream (page 109)
orange and blue colourings

to decorate, you will need

¹⁄₃ cup (50g) dark chocolate Melts, melted
¹⁄₃ cup (50g) white chocolate Melts, melted
2 chocolate bullets
3 Jaffas
80cm green Fruity Metres
40cm red Fruity Metres
2 black licorice straps
20 silver cachous

1 Grease 26cm x 36cm baking dish (base measurements), line base with baking paper. Using three packets, prepare cake mix according to directions; pour into prepared dish. Bake in moderate oven about 1 hour. Stand cake in the dish for 5 minutes; turn onto wire rack to cool.

2 Using paper pattern (see page 108), cut out dog shape; reserve leftover cake.

3 Position leftover cake at head end to complete nose. Use paper pattern to cut out nose. Place cake on board. Join nose to cake and secure with a little orange butter cream.

4 Tint two-thirds of the butter cream with orange colouring, tint remaining one-third butter cream with blue colouring. Spread top and side of cake with orange butter cream.

5 Trace outline of skateboard dog's mouth on baking paper. Turn paper over so outline is underneath. Pipe melted dark chocolate over traced lines to form mouth and teeth; leave to set.

6 Pipe melted white chocolate onto teeth, as shown; leave to set. Carefully peel mouth off baking paper and position on dog's face.

7 Spoon blue butter cream into piping bag fitted with a small plain tube; pipe spots onto dog. Position bullets for eyes and a Jaffa for the nose.

8 To make skateboard, place Fruity Metres on bench, overlapping the edges slightly; trim to form skateboard. Cut one licorice strap in half lengthways, wrap one piece around a Jaffa, continuing with second half; secure with a little butter cream. Position 10 silver cachous as shown; place wheel under skateboard. Repeat with the remaining licorice strap, Jaffa and cachous.

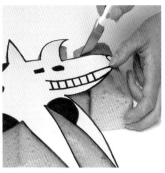

Position leftover cake at head end of paper pattern to complete nose; join nose to body with butter cream.

Pipe outline of mouth and teeth with dark chocolate; leave to set.

Pipe white chocolate into spaces for teeth; leave to set.

Wrap each half of cut licorice strap around a Jaffa, securing the end with butter cream; position cachous as shown.

Cut out the butterfly using the paper pattern as a guide.

Tint portions of butter cream with each colouring.

Following the pattern outlines as a guide, spread tinted butter creams over cake.

Position Smarties around edges of pink and blue butter cream shapes.

butterfly beauty

the glittering wings will bring a flutter to the eyes of your little girl

for the cake
3 x 340g packets buttercake mix
40cm square prepared board (page 108)
2 quantities butter cream (page 109)
violet, yellow, pink, green and blue colourings

to decorate, you will need
about 34 pink Smarties
about 26 blue Smarties
35g jar snowflakes
1 mauve chenille stick
2 lollipops

1 Grease deep 30cm square cake pan, line base with baking paper. Using three packets, prepare cake mix according to directions; pour into prepared pan. Bake in moderate oven about 1¼ hours. Stand cake in pan 10 minutes; turn onto wire rack to cool.

2 Using paper pattern (see page 108), cut out the butterfly. Place cake on board.

3 Tint one-third of the butter cream with violet colouring, and another third with yellow colouring. Divide the remaining butter cream among three bowls. Tint one portion with pink colouring, one with green colouring and one with blue.

4 Following outlines on the pattern, spread butter cream on cake.

5 Position Smarties around edges of different butter cream colours; dot all over with snowflakes. Twist chenille stick to resemble antennae; position chenille stick and lollipops as shown.

Trim about 1cm off the base edge of both cakes with a sharp knife.

the yummy yoyo

any birthday boy or girl would spin "round the world" after this spectacular bright-coloured cake

for the cake
2 x 340g packets buttercake mix
2 quantities butter cream (page 109)
green, red, blue and yellow colourings
35cm round prepared board (page 108)

to decorate, you will need
thin red licorice rope

1 Grease two deep 22cm round cake pans, line bases and sides with baking paper. Using both packets, prepare cake mix according to directions; divide between prepared pans. Bake in moderate oven about 40 minutes. Stand cakes in pans 5 minutes; turn onto wire racks to cool.
2 Using a sharp knife, trim about 1cm diagonally off the base edge of both the cakes.
3 Using a toothpick or skewer, mark top and side of each cake into six equal size swirl-shape segments.
4 Divide butter cream equally in four portions; tint one portion with red colouring, another with blue, the third with yellow, and the fourth one green.
5 Place one of the cakes, base-side up, on board. Sandwich the cakes, bases together, with green butter cream.
6 Place blue butter cream in piping bag fitted with a small plain tube; pipe into two opposing swirl-shape segments. Repeat with yellow and red butter creams. Knot the end of red licorice rope together and twist rope to make the yoyo string.

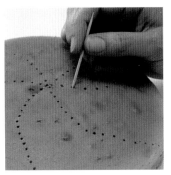
Mark the top and side of each cake into equal-sized segments with a toothpick.

Sandwich the cakes, bases together, with green butter cream.

Pipe blue, red and yellow butter cream in swirl-shaped segments over cake.

Spoon some of the pink-coloured chocolate over the doll's bodice; leave to set.

Pipe pink-coloured chocolate over outline of wings, then pipe hearts inside wings.

Pipe blue-coloured chocolate in a scrolled pattern inside the wings.

Place doll in scooped-out hole and secure with a little melted chocolate.

fairy princess

ice-cream and tinted chocolate make up the fairytale dress fit for a princess

for the princess
4 litres neapolitan ice-cream
1½ cups (225g) white chocolate Melts, melted
pink and blue colourings
40cm round prepared board (page 108)

to decorate, you will need
1 small doll
pink and gold hair mascara
silver cardboard
1 pink and 1 purple chenille sticks
2m x 5cm pink organza ribbon
2m x 5cm blue organza ribbon

1 Grease a 20cm Dolly Varden pan (2.5 Litre/10-cup capacity), line with plastic wrap, extending plastic about 5cm over edge of pan.
2 Separate vanilla, strawberry and chocolate ice-cream into three bowls. Using a slotted spoon, press down on ice-cream until just soft. Scoop alternate spoonfuls of each colour into pan. Tap pan on bench to settle ice-cream; cover with foil, freeze overnight.
3 Remove legs from doll, colour hair with mascara. Separate the melted chocolate into two bowls; tint half the chocolate with pink colouring and half with blue. Using a spoon, coat bodice area of the doll's body with some of the pink chocolate. Tap doll on the bench to smooth out chocolate; leave to set.
4 Trace outline of wings on baking paper. Turn paper over so outline is underneath. Pipe pink chocolate over traced lines to form wings and hearts; leave to set.
5 Pipe blue chocolate in a scrolled pattern inside wings; leave to set. Pipe a little of the remaining blue chocolate in a decorative pattern onto the doll's pink bodice.
6 Carefully peel the wings from the baking paper. Supporting wings between two bowls, join them together with pink chocolate; leave to set.
7 To make wand, cut three small stars out of the silver cardboard. Cut pink chenille stick 10cm long; fix one end between the stars. Using purple chenille stick, make a crown, secure around the doll's head.
8 Remove ice-cream from pan, place on board. Using a teaspoon, scoop out a small hole in the top of the ice-cream; secure doll in hole with little melted chocolate. Drizzle pink and blue chocolate over ice-cream in a decorative pattern to make doll's skirt; return to freezer until set. Tie ribbon into a bow around doll's waist. Attach wings to doll's back with a little chocolate; return to freezer until required.

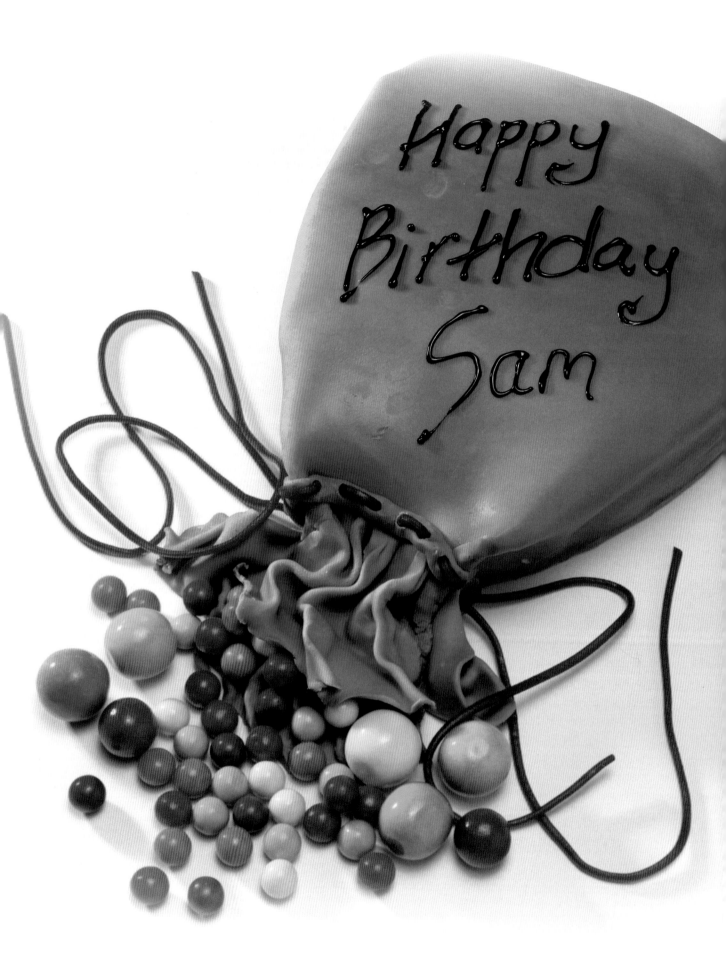

Happy Birthday Sam

marble bag

the birthday guests will all lose their marbles over this ingenious bag of tricks

for the cake
2 x 340g packets buttercake mix
3 cups (450g) white chocolate Melts, melted
blue colouring
¼ cup (60ml) light corn syrup
35cm x 40cm rectangular prepared board (page 108)
¼ cup (60ml) apricot jam, warmed, sieved
icing sugar

to decorate, you will need
3 x 60cm pieces thin red licorice rope
gum balls of assorted sizes and colours
black decorating gel

1 Grease deep 25cm round cake pan, line base with baking paper. Using both packets, prepare cake mix according to directions; pour into prepared pan. Bake in moderate oven about 1 hour. Stand cake in pan for 5 minutes; turn onto wire rack to cool.

2 Tint melted chocolate with blue colouring; add some corn syrup, stir until mixture thickens and becomes slightly grainy. Cover; stand at room temperature about 1 hour or until mixture is firm.

3 Using paper pattern (see page 108), cut out the marble bag. Place cake, base-side up, on the board.

4 Using a sharp knife, slightly trim top of cake at an angle towards "opening" of the marble bag. Brush top and sides of cakes evenly with warm jam.

5 On a surface dusted with icing sugar, knead blue chocolate mixture until smooth and soft. Roll out on a sheet of baking paper until large enough to cover top and side of cake. Carefully place chocolate on cake, press firmly around side of cake, trim around edge (except for the bag's opening); reserve any leftover chocolate mixture.

6 Gently ease the chocolate mixture around the bag's opening into decorative folds. Re-roll reserved excess chocolate mixture; place in folds around opening to make a double layer, trim to neaten edges. Roll a sausage shape about 10cm long from chocolate trimmings; press over joins of decorative folds.

7 Using a skewer or a toothpick, pierce holes about 1.5cm apart on the bag's opening; press short pieces of licorice into holes to look like stitched-in drawstring. Bend two 60cm pieces of licorice in half and attach to side of opening to resemble the pulls on drawstrings. Place the gum balls in position and pipe a message on the bag with decorating gel.

Slightly trim the top of the cake at an angle towards the opening of the bag.

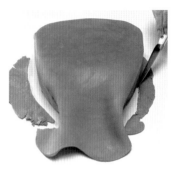

Trim excess blue-coloured chocolate mixture from base of cake, leaving top of bag for opening.

Create folds in chocolate mixture around bag's opening; make more folds from chocolate scraps and place in opening.

Press short pieces of red licorice into marked holes to create drawstring stitches.

kindy blocks

as simple as a-b-c, you can count on the nursery set adoring these cakes

for the cake

4 x 340g buttercake mix
3 quantities butter cream (page 109)
pink, sky blue and yellow colourings
35cm square prepared board (page 108)

to decorate, you will need

3 yellow musk sticks
3 pink musk sticks
3 green musk sticks
¾ cup (105g) white chocolate Melts, melted
yellow, blue and pink sugar crystals

Level tops of cakes with a serrated knife, so that one cake is 5cm high and the other is 6cm high.

Sandwich a 5cm- and 6cm-high square together with butter cream.

Pipe melted chocolate into numbers and letters on marked baking paper.

Before chocolate sets, sprinkle different coloured sugar crystals over numbers and letters.

1 Grease two deep 23cm square cake pans, line bases with baking paper. Using the four packets, prepare cake mix according to directions; divide between prepared pans. Bake in moderate oven for about 1 hour. Stand cakes in pans 5 minutes; turn onto wire racks to cool.

2 Using a serrated knife, level tops of cakes so that one is 5cm high and the other cake is 6cm high. Cut each cake into four squares.

3 Tint one-third of the butter cream with pink colouring, another third with blue and remainder with yellow.

4 Sandwich a 5cm- and 6cm-high square with some butter cream. Repeat until you have three 11cm cubes. (There will be one piece of each thickness of cake left over.) Spread each block with a different colour butter cream. Arrange blocks on the board.

5 Cut each musk stick lengthways into four even-size strips; outline all edges of blocks with musk sticks.

6 Pipe melted chocolate numbers and letters on baking paper.

7 Before chocolate sets, sprinkle with sugar crystals; leave to set. Carefully peel numbers and letter off baking paper and position on blocks.

tropical turtle

**who could resist the tropical turtle
with her yummy chocolate shell?**

*Spoon cream mixture on top of cake
to form a dome on the turtle's back.*

for the cake

3 x 340g packets buttercake mix
35cm x 45cm rectangular prepared board (page 108)
300ml thickened cream
½ cup (125ml) strawberry jam
2 quantities butter cream (page 109)
green, pink and red colourings
1 cup (150g) white chocolate Melts, melted

to decorate, you will need

1 white marshmallow
blue and black decorating gel
thin red licorice rope

*Using a toothpick, swirl through patches
of pink and red chocolate to create a
marbling effect.*

1 Grease 26cm x 32cm baking dish (base measurements), line base with baking paper. Using three packets, prepare cake mix according to directions; pour into prepared dish. Bake in moderate oven about 45 minutes. Stand cake in dish 5 minutes; turn onto wire rack to cool.

2 Using paper pattern (see page 108), cut out the turtle's body and the single flipper as shown; reserve leftover cake pieces. Place cake on the board.

3 Beat cream in small bowl with electric mixer until soft peaks form. Chop reserved leftover cake into 2cm pieces; fold pieces and jam into cream. Spoon cream mixture on top of cake to form the dome of the turtle's back.

*Once chocolate has set, break into
pieces; position onto turtle's back.*

4 Divide butter cream between two bowls; tint half of the butter cream dark green and the other half light green. Spread top of the cake and cream mixture with light green butter cream; spread the dark green butter cream around feet, flippers, head and side of cake.

5 Hand-draw an approximate-size outline of the turtle's back on baking paper; turn paper over. Divide the melted chocolate between two bowls; tint half of chocolate with pink colouring and the other half red. Pour both tinted chocolates, in patches, onto baking paper within the marks of the outline. Using a toothpick or skewer, swirl the chocolate patches together, marbling the pink and red into a tortoise-shell pattern. Leave to set; break into pieces.

6 Press chocolate pieces onto the turtle's back, as shown.

7 To make eyes, cut marshmallow in half; pipe dots with blue and black gel to complete eyes, position on head. Use red licorice to create mouth. Pipe wavy lines on board with blue gel to represent flowing water.

*Pipe dots of blue and black decorating
gel onto cut marshmallows to make
the eyes.*

Pile crushed pavlova over top of pavlova shell to make a dome.

Spread whipped cream mixture all over crushed pavlovas to cover dome completely.

Position marshmallows over dome, pressing gently into cream mixture.

Wrap shortened flower stems with parafilm tape.

flower bombe

a flounce of pastel flowers makes this extravagant bouquet

Packaged pavlova shells are available from most supermarkets. Use flowers of your choice if lisianthus and tuberoses are not in season. Parafilm tape, used in floral arrangements, is available from florists or specialty stores.

for the cake
3 x 500g purchased pavlova shells
35cm round prepared board (page 108)
600ml thickened cream
2 tablespoons icing sugar

to decorate, you will need
200g large pink and white marshmallows
1 cup (70g) shredded coconut
8 pink lisianthus
8 white lisianthus
8 tuberoses
parafilm tape
silver cachous
1m pink organza ribbon
1m silver organza ribbon

1 Place pavlova shell on board. Crush remaining two pavlova shells; pile over top to form a dome.
2 Beat cream and icing sugar in medium bowl with electric mixer until soft peak form. Spread cream over top of crushed pavlovas.
3 Press marshmallows into cream; sprinkle with coconut.
4 Shorten flower stems to about 5cm length; wrap stems with tape. Position flowers in between marshmallows all over cake. Dust cake with a little sifted icing sugar; scatter silver cachous over cake. Tie one ribbon into a bow; tie remaining ribbon around base of the cake, attach the bow to the front.

clowning around

everyone loves a clown and this winning face is sure to charm the partygoers

Cut one large triangle for the hat and two small triangles for the bow-tie from square cake.

for the cake
3 x 340g packets buttercake mix
2 quantities butter cream (page 109)
red, green, blue and yellow colourings
30cm x 60cm rectangular prepared board (page 108)

to decorate, you will need
100g packet Chang's fried noodles
1 black licorice strap
thin red licorice rope
1 large red gum ball
1 large yellow gum ball
11 small gum balls in assorted colours

Place round cake and hat on board, then position the smaller triangles for the bow-tie.

1 Grease deep 19cm square and deep 22cm round cake pans, line bases with baking paper. Using three packets, prepare cake mix according to directions; divide between prepared pans. Bake cakes in moderate oven about 1 hour. Stand cakes in pans 5 minutes; turn onto wire racks to cool.

2 Place half of the butter cream, untinted, in a medium bowl; reserve. Place 2 tablespoons of the remaining butter cream in a small bowl; tint with red colouring. Divide remaining butter cream into two small bowls; tint one portion with green colouring and the other with blue.

3 If necessary, level top of cakes so they are of the same height, using a serrated knife. Mark halfway point on to edge of square cake; cut from halfway point to bottom corners to form a large triangle hat. Cut two even-sided triangles from remaining corners of square cake; there will be leftover cake.

Shake noodles in plastic bag with colouring until evenly coloured.

4 Place round cake, base-side up, on board; position cake triangles as shown.

5 Spread clown with white, green and blue butter cream.

6 Place noodles in small plastic bag with a few drops of yellow colouring; shake well. When noodles are dry, place around face for hair.

7 Cut small pieces of licorice for each eye and eyebrow; place in position. Outline smile with red licorice; spread red butter cream inside smile, repeat with cheeks. Place a small half-circle of black licorice inside smile. Position large gum balls for nose and bow-tie "knot"; place the smaller gum balls on the hat. Outline bow-tie with red licorice; make a three-petalled daisy at top of hat with red licorice and a gum ball.

Place black licorice strips for eyes and lashes; outline a mouth with red licorice, then fill with butter cream.

Knead half of the willow green icing with half of the kelly green icing to make a fourth green colour.

Cut out gum leaf shapes from each green-tinted portion of icing with a small sharp knife.

Shape wombat bodies from brown icing, koalas from the grey icing and possums from the grey-brown icing.

Colour wombats' and koalas' noses with non-toxic black pen; pipe pink decorating gel on possums' noses.

bush babies

it's easy to make an authentically Australian menagerie – hide them in a deluge of fallen gum leaves

for the cake
2 x 340g packets buttercake mix
30cm round prepared board (page 108)
1½ quantities chocolate butter cream (page 109)
icing sugar
500g packet ready-made soft icing
juniper green, kelly green, willow green, brown and black food colourings

to decorate, you will need
white and pink decorating gel
non-toxic black felt-tipped pen
60cm x 3.5cm sheer gold ribbon

1 Grease deep 22cm round cake pan, line base with baking paper. Using two packets, prepare cake mix according to directions; pour into prepared pan. Bake in moderate oven about 1 hour. Stand cake in pan for 5 minutes; turn onto wire rack to cool. Using a serrated knife, level top of cake. Place cake, base-side up, on board; spread top and side with butter cream.

2 On a surface dusted with icing sugar, knead icing until smooth and pliable. Divide icing into thirds; cover two-thirds of the icing with plastic wrap; pressing plastic down firmly onto the surface of icing to prevent it drying out, reserve. Tint one quarter of the remaining icing with juniper green colouring; tint half of the remaining icing with willow green colouring; tint the rest with kelly green colouring. Knead half of the willow green icing and half of the kelly green icing together to make a fourth green colour. Wrap each ball of icing individually in plastic wrap to prevent them drying out.

3 On a surface dusted with icing sugar, roll out the four individual icing balls about 2mm thick. Using a small sharp knife, cut out gum leaf shapes; reroll scraps to cut out more leaf shapes. Twist leaves slightly; drape over edge of pan to dry.

4 On a surface dusted with icing sugar, tint half of the reserved two-thirds of the icing a wombat colour with brown colouring; tint the remaining half a grey koala colour using the black colouring. Cut off about a third of each of the two colours; knead together to make a third grey-brown colour possum colour.

5 Divide brown icing in half, reserving a little to make the wombats' noses. Shape two wombat bodies; make a small cut under each chin, pinch together to shape each head. Pinch sides of head to make ears; use a skewer to make eyes. Divide grey icing into quarters, reserving a little to make the koalas' eyes and noses. Shape two koala bodies and two heads; attach heads to bodies using a little water. Divide grey-brown colour into quarters, reserving a little to make possums' eyes and noses. Shape two possum bodies and two heads; attach heads to bodies using a little water.

6 Finish animals by rolling reserved three colours of icing into tiny balls for eyes and noses; attach using a little water. Use a skewer to make pupils for eyes, nostrils and mouths. Colour wombats' and koalas' noses with non-toxic black pen; colour possums' noses with pink decorating gel. Arrange leaves on top of the cake; place animals on top of leaves. Wrap ribbon around side of cake, tie into bow.

purr-fect friend

**if the birthday person is mad about cats,
this enigmatic creation will be... purrfection**

for the cake
3 x 340g packets buttercake mix
35cm x 45cm rectangular prepared board (page 108)
2 quantities butter cream (page 109)
black colouring

to decorate, you will need
3 marshmallows
2 black licorice straps
pink and black decorating gel
2 green M&M's
2 white chocolate Melts
1 x 140g packet thin red licorice rope

1 Grease 26cm x 36cm baking dish (base measurements), line base with baking paper. Using three packets, prepare cake mix according to directions; pour into prepared dish. Bake in moderate oven about 1 hour. Stand cake in dish for 5 minutes; turn onto wire rack to cool.

2 Using paper pattern (see page 108), cut out cat. Place cake on board. Mark out head and tail with toothpick or skewer.

3 Cut one marshmallow into four pieces; position on face for cheeks, chin and nose. Place one marshmallow on each paw.

4 Reserve one-quarter of the butter cream. Tint remaining butter cream grey with black colouring.

5 Spread body with grey butter cream. Spread head marking, eyes, chest and stripe with white butter cream.

6 Dot tail with grey butter cream to make stripes. Using fork, blend butter cream on back and tail stripes; fluff butter cream with a fork to resemble fur.

7 Cut one licorice strap into thin stirps; outline body, tail, head, ears, eyes and paws with licorice. Pipe nose with pink decorating gel. Pipe mouth with black gel. Cut remaining licorice into six 3cm strips; attach for whiskers. Press M&M's into butter cream for eyes; mark pupils with black decorating gel. Cut white chocolate melts into quarters, use three pieces for claws on each paw. Roll the licorice rope into a "ball of yarn", and stick two skewer or chopsticks into it, if desired.

Position marshmallow quarters on face for nose, cheeks and chin, then place marshmallows on cake for paws.

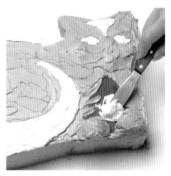

Spread grey butter cream over cake for body and white butter cream for head marking, eyes, chest and stripe.

Blend dots of grey butter cream into white tail to create stripes.

Outline cat body and features with licorice strips, then pipe pink decorating gel on face for nose.

waving the flag

**strike a patriotic note with one
of these berry imaginative creations**

for the cake

**(the quantities given for cake, cream and berries
    are enough to make one flag.)**
3 x 340g packets buttercake mix
600ml thickened cream
35cm x 45cm rectangular prepared board (page 108)

to decorate, you will need
British flag:
1.25kg strawberries
750g blueberries
Canadian flag:
1.5kg strawberries
Australian flag:
500g strawberries
1.5kg blueberries
1 cup (150g) white chocolate Melts, melted

1 Grease 26cm x 36cm baking dish (base measurements),
   line base with baking paper. Using three packets,
   prepares cake mix according to directions; pour into
   prepared dish. Bake in moderate oven about 1 hour.
   Stand cake in dish for 5 minutes; turn onto wire rack
   to cool. Place cake, base-side up, on board.

2 Beat cream in medium bowl with electric mixer until
   soft peaks form. Spread cake with cream. Place berries
   on cake for desired flag, as shown, trimming and slicing
   the strawberries where necessary. For the Australian flag
   cake, place white chocolate stars (see step 3) on top to
   form the Southern Cross.

3 To make the chocolate stars, spread melted white
   chocolate on a sheet of baking paper. When chocolate
   is almost set, cut out stars with a knife.

GREAT BRITAIN

CANADA

AUSTRALIA

team fever

a cake in shape of a football jersey — decorate it
with the colours of your child's favourite team
to make him the hero of the day

for the cake
4 x 340g packets buttercake mix
40cm x 60cm rectangular prepared board (page 108)
2 quantities butter cream (page 109)
yellow and blue colouring
²/₃ cup (100g) white chocolate Melts, melted

to decorate, you will need
130g tube red Fruity Metres
130g tube green Fruity Metres
black decorating gel
blue and yellow candy letter decorations

1 Grease two 26cm x 32cm baking dishes (base measurements), line bases with baking paper. Using four packets, prepare cake mix according to directions; divide mixture evenly among prepared dishes. Bake in moderate oven about 35 minutes. Stand cake in dishes 5 minutes; turn onto wire racks to cool.

2 Using paper pattern (see page 108), cut out half the jersey, turn pattern and cut out other half. Place cakes on board.

3 Tint butter cream with yellow colouring. Spread top and side of the cake with butter cream.

4 Cut and position red and green Fruity Metres as shown.

5 To make happy birthday and number plaques, make outlines of a 4cm x 16cm rectangle and 5.5mm circle on baking paper. Tint melted chocolate with blue colouring. Spread chocolate within the rectangle and circle outlines; when chocolate is almost set, trim edges; peel off paper.

6 Using decorating gel, pipe on plaques. Carefully lift and position plaques on cake. Press candy letters onto sleeves of jersey, as desired.

Cut out half the jersey on one cake using pattern as a guide; turn over pattern and cut out another half.

Decorate Jersey with strips of red and green Fruity Metres on sleeves, collar and hem.

Spread blue-tinted chocolate on marked baking paper to make 'happy birthday' and number plaques.

Pipe birthday message and number on plaques with black decorating gel.

soccer ball

for the cake

3 x 340g packets buttercake mix
30cm round prepared board (page 108)
2 quantities butter cream (page 109)

to decorate, you will need

1¹⁄₃ cups (200g) dark chocolate Melts, melted
1 black licorice strap

1 Grease two large 2.25-Litre (9-cup) capacity pudding steamers. Using three packets, prepare cake mix according to directions; pour into prepared steamers. Beak in moderate oven about one hour. Stand cakes in steamers 5 minutes; turn onto wire racks to cool.

2 Using a serrated knife, level tops of cakes; sandwich together on board with butter cream. Spread the cake with remaining butter cream.

3 Spread melted chocolate about 2mm thick on baking paper. Using the paper pattern supplied, left, cut out chocolate hexagons.

4 Cut licorice into thin 2.5cm long strips. Place chocolate hexagons, base-side up, and licorice strips, in hexagonal patterns, all over cake.

Sandwich cakes together with some butter cream, then spread remaining butter cream all over cake.

Using pattern below as a guide, cut hexagon shapes from chocolate.

Place chocolate hexagons and licorice strips over cakes to create ball pattern.

SOCCER BALL PATTERN

Push a long wooden skewer through the joined cakes.

Using decorating gel, pipe black lines along the length of the ball and white stitches across the black lines.

rugby ball

for the cake
3 x 340g packets buttercake mix
2 quantities butter cream (page 109)
30cm x 40cm rectangular prepared board (page 108)

to decorate, you will need
black and white decorating gel
green and yellow Fruity Metres
thin red licorice rope
½ cup (100g) chocolate thins

Using green and yellow Fruity Metres, make a crest for the birthday message.

1 Grease two 20cm Dolly Varden pans (2.5-Litre/10-cup capacity). Make cakes according to directions on packets; pour into prepared pans. Bake in moderate oven 1¼ hours. Stand cakes 5 minutes; turn onto wire racks to cool.

2 Using a serrated knife, level tops of cakes; cut a small section off a side of one cake to give a level base. Securing with a long skewer, sandwich cakes together with butter cream on board. Cover cake with butter cream.

3 Using black decorating gel, mark lines along length of ball; mark out an oval on top of cake. Use white decorating gel to indicate stitches.

4 Using Fruity Metres, make a green and yellow crest. Using black decorating gel, pipe desired message on crest. Position crest on side of ball.

5 Cut six 4cm lengths of red licorice; bend licorice pieces into "laces" and position on top of cake. Make a small pump hole with licorice and position on cake. Sprinkle chocolate thins around base of ball.

Using short lengths of red licorice, bend "laces" into position on top of cake.

Add a few drops of red and blue colouring to the green butter cream to make a deeper green colour.

Sprinkle top of cake with green sugar crystals.

Spoon yellow jelly crystals inside cardboard template for pitch.

cricket pitch

for the cricket pitch cake
3 x 340g packets buttercake mix
1 quantity butter cream (page 109)
green, red and blue colourings
40cm x 45cm rectangular prepared board (page 108)

to decorate, you will need
¹/₃ cup (65g) green sugar crystals
3 teaspoons yellow jelly crystals
toy cricket players and stumps

1 Grease deep 31cm oval cake pan, line base with baking paper. Using three packets, prepare cake mix according to directions; pour into prepared pan. Bake in moderate oven about 1½ hours. Stand cake in pan 5 minutes; turn onto wire rack to cool. Using a serrated knife, level top of cake.
2 Tint butter cream with green colouring, then carefully add a few drops of red and blue colourings, to result in a rich, deep green colour.
3 Place cake, base-side up, on board. Spread top and side of cake with butter cream; sprinkle top of cake with green sugar crystals.
4 Cut a 4cm x 15cm rectangle out of a piece of cardboard. Place cardboard on cake, sprinkle yellow jelly crystals inside piece of cardboard. Gently lift cardboard off cake. Position players and stumps on cake.

tennis court

for the tennis court cake

3 x 340g packets buttercake mix
1 quantity butter cream (page 109)
500g packet ready-made soft icing
caramel, terracotta, brown and royal blue colourings
35cm x 45cm rectangular prepared board (page 108)
icing sugar

to decorate, you will need

2m x 2mm wide white ribbon
1 egg white
20cm netting
6 toothpicks
½ cup (70g) white chocolate Melts, melted
3 x black licorice straps
2 pieces thin red licorice rope
¼ cup (35g) dark chocolate Melts, melted
30cm strip strawberry flavoured Fruity Metres
4 small mints

1 Grease 26cm x 36cm baking dish (base measurements), line base with baking paper. Using three packets, prepare cake mix according to directions; pour into prepared dish. Bake in moderate oven about 1 hour. Stand cake in dish for 5 minutes; turn onto wire rack to cool.

2 Tint butter cream with caramel, terracotta and brown colourings. Place cake, base-side up, on prepared board; spread cake with butter cream.

3 On a surface dusted with icing sugar, knead icing until smooth and pliable. Tint icing with blue colouring; knead until colour is evenly distributed. Wrap tightly in plastic; stand until firm, 1 hour or overnight.

4 On a sheet of baking paper dusted with icing sugar, roll out icing evenly to a piece large enough in area to cut out a 15cm x 32.5cm rectangle. Carefully place icing on centre of cake. Cut ribbon into four 32.5cm, two 11.6cm, two 15cm and one 17.4cm lengths. Brush backs of ribbons lightly with egg white; press onto court as shown. Secure net onto cake with toothpicks. To make the happy birthday signs, pipe melted chocolate on 10cm pieces of black licorice. Join two pieces of licorice together with chocolate and outline with red rope licorice. Position on cake. To make umpire's chair, cut two 2cm pieces of licorice strap. On each corner of one piece of licorice, attach four toothpicks. Push two toothpicks through licorice and attach other piece of licorice. Position the chair on the cake.

5 Draw four tennis racquets on paper and pipe melted dark chocolate to fill in outline. Pipe racquet strings with melted white chocolate. When set, peel off paper and wrap narrow strips of Fruity Metres around racquet handles. Position on cake along small mints for balls.

Spread brown-coloured butter cream over top and sides of cake.

Knead blue colouring into icing on icing-sugar-dusted surface until evenly distributed.

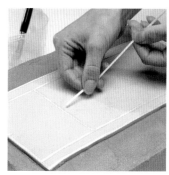

Brush various lengths of white ribbon with a little egg white, then place onto court as shown.

Pipe dark chocolate racquets on baking paper, pipe strings with white chocolate; wrap Fruity Metres around handles.

fields of play

We've included these diagrams to help start you on your way to achieving the look of your child's favourite playing field, but feel free to lash out with your own embellishments – after all, the only limits imposed on creating a personalised cake are those set by your imagination.

We covered the top of this cake with green sprinkles and sugar crystals, piped the in-goal areas and metre lines with white decorating icing, made goal posts out of Fruity Metres wrapped around lollipop sticks, and piped the numbers with melted white chocolate.

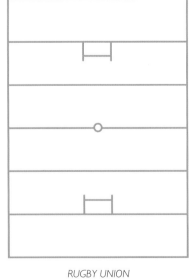

RUGBY UNION

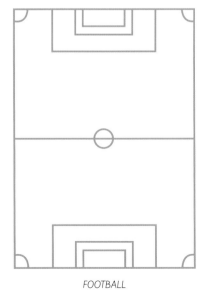

FOOTBALL

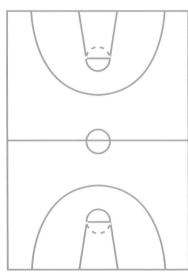

BASKETBALL

Cut out skull from one cake using pattern as a guide; cut out rounds and rectangles from remaining cake.

Position cake pieces on the board, making crossbones with cake rectangles and rounds.

skull and crossbones

ahoy there! let the birthday child head for the high seas with this pirate creation

for the cake
3 x 340g packets buttercake mix
3 quantities fluffy frosting (see page 106)
40cm x 50cm rectangular prepared board (page 108)

to decorate, you will need
2 egg shell halves
red colouring or non-toxic red pan
2 brown Smarties
1 licorice strap
bullets

1 Grease two 20cm x 30cm lamington pans, line bases with baking paper. Using three packets, prepare cake mix according to directions; divide between prepared pans. Bake in moderate oven for about 40 minutes; turn onto wire racks to cool.

2 Using paper pattern (see page 108), cut out skull from one cake. Cut out eight 2cm rounds for ends of bones and four rectangles for bones from remaining cake.

3 Position cake pieces on board, join with a little frosting. Cover cake pieces with remaining frosting.

4 Using red colouring, mark lines in shell halves for veins, place a Smartie in the centre. Cut out nose from the licorice strap and place on face. Cut bullets in half lengthways and place on cake for teeth.

pony perfect

perfect for the little girl who dreams
of having her very own pony

for the cake

2 x 340g packets buttercake mix
2 quantities butter cream (page 109)
brown colouring
40cm square prepared board (page 108)

to decorate, you will need

2 licorice straps
1 chocolate freckle
1 lifesaver

1 Grease two 20cm x 30cm lamington pans, line bases with baking paper.
   Using two packets, make cake according to directions; divide mixture
   between pans. Bake in moderate oven for about 30 minutes; turn onto
   wire racks to cool.
2 Place cakes side-by-side; using paper pattern (see page 108) cut out pony.
3 Position cakes on board, join with a little butter cream. Tint two-thirds of
   remaining butter cream brown, spread evenly over cake, except for mane.
   Use remaining untinted cream for mane.
4 Cut pieces from licorice strap for eye and nostril; cut licorice strap into thin
   strips for bridle, then position on cake with freckle and lifesaver as shown.

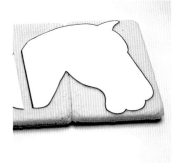

*Position cakes side-by-side, then cut out
pony using pattern as a guide.*

*Assemble cake pieces on prepared
board, joining together with a little
butter cream.*

BASIC KNOW-HOW

We used packet cake mixes throughout this book to ensure consistency of size and texture. However, if you would prefer to make your own cake, we have included four fabulously easy and delicious recipes in these information pages to use as your starting point.

MAKING THE CAKE

For best results:

- Use an electric mixer when beating the cake mixture
- Follow the directions on the packet
- Have all ingredients at room temperature
- A large mixing bowl should have the capacity to hold 4 packet mixes. It's best to mix single packets in a small bowl, and 2 or 3 packets in a medium bowl

BAKING CAKES TOGETHER

You can bake cakes together, either on the same oven shelf or on different shelves. The important thing is that the cake pans do not touch each other, the sides of the oven or the door. If baking cakes on the same shelf, exchange the positions of the pans about halfway through baking time.

If baking cakes on different shelves, make certain there is enough room for the cake on the lower shelf to rise without touching the bottom of the shelf above it. Change the cakes from the lower to the upper shelf positions about halfway through baking time for even browning.

When small cakes are baked with larger cakes (which have longer baking times), place the small ones toward the front of the oven then, when the small cakes are baked, move the large cakes into that position to complete their baking time.

When two or more cakes are being baked in the oven at the same time, the baking time may be slightly longer than specified in recipes. A perfectly baked cake should feel firm to the touch and be slightly shrunken from the side(s) of the pan. There should not be any need to test with a skewer. However, if in doubt, test by inserting a metal skewer into the centre of the cake; if any mixture clings to the skewer, the cake needs a little more baking time. Never test a sponge cake with a skewer; instead, gently press the surface of cake with fingertips – it should feel firm.

CAKE PANS

Each recipe specifies the required pan size(s) and exact quantities required to make your cakes look the same as ours. However, cake sizes and shapes can be changed to suit yourself and your chosen decorations.

Use rigid, straight-sided, deep cake pans. The ones we used are made from good quality tin or aluminium.

GREASING AND LINING THE CAKE PAN

All cake pans were greased lightly but evenly with a pastry brush dipped in a little melted butter. An alternative method is to spray pans with cooking-oil spray. We lined the bases of the pans with baking paper. To fit baking paper, place the pan, right-side up, on a piece of baking paper, then trace around the pan's base with a pencil. Cut the paper shape just slightly inside the marked area, to allow for the thickness of the pan. We also lined the side(s) of the cake pans so the paper extended above the edge of the pan by about 5cm.

To line base of cake pan with baking paper trace around the base of the pan.

A paper collar extending approximately 5cm above pan will ensure the cake will not brown too much.

CAKE RECIPES

Each of these recipes makes a cake equal in quantity to one 340g packet of buttercake cake mix. Therefore, if the particular recipe you've decided to make calls for two packets of cake mix, double the quantities called for and adjust the baking time. These four cake recipes will bake in approximately the same time as the packet mixes.

BASIC BUTTER CAKE

125g butter, softened
1 teaspoon vanilla extract
¾ cup (165g) caster sugar
2 eggs
1½ cups (225g) self-raising flour
½ cup (125ml) milk

Preheat oven to moderate. Grease (and line) pan(s).
Beat butter, extract and sugar in small bowl with electric mixer until light and fluffy. Beat in eggs, one at a time, until combined. Stir in sifted flour and milk, in two batches. Spread mixture into prepared pan(s). Bake in moderate oven until cake is cooked. Stand cake in pan(s) about 5 minutes; turn onto wire rack to cool.
To marble a butter cake, place portions of cake mixture in different bowls then tint each with desired colour. Dollop spoonfuls of mixture into prepared pan(s), alternating colours, then gently swirl together with a skewer or spoon, to create marbled effect.

RICH CHOCOLATE CAKE

1⅓ cups (200g) self-raising flour
½ cup (50g) cocoa powder
125g butter, softened
1 teaspoon vanilla extract
1¼ cups (275g) caster sugar
2 eggs
⅔ cup (160ml) water

Preheat oven to moderate. Grease (and line) pan(s).
Sift flour and cocoa into medium bowl, add remaining ingredients; beat on low speed with electric mixer until ingredients are combined. Increase speed to medium; beat about 3 minutes or until mixture is smooth and changed to a lighter colour. Spread into prepared pan(s). Bake in moderate oven until cake is cooked. Stand cake in pan(s) about 5 minutes; turn onto wire rack to cool.

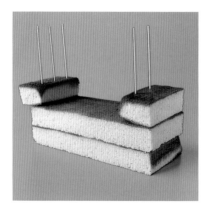

Wooden skewers are often used to secure cake pieces in place.

Use a serrated knife to neaten edges of a square cake.

BEST-EVER SPONGE

The only liquid called for in this recipe comes from the eggs; for best results, they should be at room temperature.

3 eggs
½ cup (110g) caster sugar
¼ cup (35g) cornflour
¼ cup (35g) plain flour
¼ cup (35g) self-raising flour

Preheat oven to moderate. Grease (and line) pan(s). Beat eggs in small bowl with electric mixer until thick and creamy (this will take about 8 minutes). Add sugar, 1 tablespoon at a time, beating after each addition, until sugar dissolves; transfer mixture to large bowl. Sift dry ingredients together three times then sift evenly over egg mixture; fold in gently. Spread into prepared pan(s). Bake in moderate oven until cake is cooked. Turn immediately onto wire rack to cool.

WHEAT-FREE SPONGE

This is a gluten-free cake, for people who suffer from coeliac disease and do not tolerate wheat flour. Cornflour, also called cornstarch in some countries, is made from corn kernels and contains no gluten. Use care when purchasing cornflour because there is a wheaten cornflour available which, as the name suggests, contains wheat.

3 eggs
½ cup (110g) caster sugar
¾ cup (110g) cornflour (100% corn)

Preheat oven to moderate. Grease (and line) pan(s). Beat eggs in small bowl with electric mixer until thick and creamy (this will take about 8 minutes). Add sugar, 1 tablespoon at a time, beating after each addition until sugar dissolves. Sift cornflour three times then sift evenly over egg mixture; fold in gently. Spread into prepared pan(s). Bake in moderate oven until cake is cooked. Turn immediately onto wire rack to cool.

Use a very sharp knife to trim cake into neat shapes.

Use a serrated knife to level the rounded top of a cake.

PREPARING THE CAKE(S)

Trim cooked cake(s) so it sits flat or joins neatly to another cake. Most cakes in this book use the smooth base as the top of the finished cake; in this case, it's a good idea to cool the cake upside down. Some cakes are decorated top-side up.

Crumbs can present problems when they become mixed with the icing. To prevent this from happening, bake cake the day before you decorate it. After the cake cools, keep it in an airtight container in the refrigerator overnight. Decorate cake while it is still cold. If you think you will take longer than 30 minutes to decorate the cake, freeze it, uncovered, for 30 minutes, before decorating.

CAKE BOARDS

Some of the cakes in this book call for a cake board which becomes part of the decoration. In any case, the board makes the cake easy to handle as well as more attractive.

Place cake(s), as directed, on a board that has been covered with greaseproof decorative paper, contact, or any type of patterned foil-like gift wrapping. We've given an approximate cake-board size in almost all of the recipes, allowing some space around the cake. Using masonite or a similarly strong board, cut the selected paper 5cm to 10cm larger than the shape of the board. A variety of sizes of boards can be bought, already covered in paper, from cake-decorating suppliers and some craft shops.

USING PAPER PATTERNS

THE PATTERNS SUPPLIED FOR CAKES ON THE PATTERN SHEET ARE OF ACTUAL SIZE.

If you choose to make a cake that is based on a pattern, you will find the template on the pattern sheet in the back of this book. Using a pencil, trace the pattern onto baking or greaseproof paper. Carefully cut around this paper tracing. Assemble cake pieces as directed in the recipe method, then place the paper pattern on top of cake. Using toothpicks, secure pattern onto cake. Using a small serrated knife, cut around the pattern to form the shape of the cake. Remove toothpicks and pattern, then proceed with the recipe.

If cutting shapes from ready-made soft icing using a paper pattern, use the above method but do not use toothpicks to secure the pattern to icing. Use a small sharp-pointed knife to cut around the pattern.

To cover square or rectangular boards, fold paper neatly at the corners and glue or tape securely to the underside of the board.

For round boards, snip paper at intervals, as shown, then fold over and glue or tape securely to the underside of the board.

Secure paper pattern to cake with toothpicks; cut around shape using small pointed sharp, or serrated, knife.

CHOOSING THE ICING

We used either ready-made soft icing, butter cream or fluffy frosting, depending on the effect we desired. Ready-made soft icing is easy to use and gives a smooth surface to the cake. Butter cream is a little harder to spread than fluffy frosting, but you can work with butter cream longer than with fluffy frosting, which tends to set. Fluffy frosting is good for fluffy or snowy effects, but it is fairly difficult to make smooth.

The yellow colour of the butter cream will affect the colour you choose. For example, if you add rose pink, the cream tends to become salmon pink; if you add red, it becomes apricot and so on. If you use ready-made soft icing or fluffy frosting, you have a white base to colour from.

Use a spatula or palette knife for spreading and swirling butter cream or fluffy frosting.

READY-MADE SOFT ICING

Ready-made soft icing can be bought from cake-decorating suppliers and some health food shops, delicatessens and supermarkets. There are several brands available, and they can be sold as Soft Icing, Prepared Icing or Ready to Roll Icing. All are easy to handle; knead the icing gently on a surface dusted with sifted icing sugar until it is smooth.

Brush warmed strained apricot jam lightly and evenly all over cake. Roll icing until it is about 7mm thick. Lift icing onto cake with rolling pin. Smooth the icing with hands dusted with icing sugar, easing it around the side(s) and base of cake. Push icing in around the base of cake then cut away any excess with a sharp knife.

BUTTER CREAM

This is a basic butter cream (also known as vienna cream) recipe; the flavour can be varied by adding different flavoured extracts, such as banana, orange, mint, etc.

125g butter, softened
1½ cups (240g) icing sugar
2 tablespoons milk

Beat butter in small bowl with electric mixer until as white as possible. Gradually beat in half of the sifted icing sugar, milk, then remaining sifted icing sugar. Flavour and colour as required.

Chocolate variation: Sift ⅓ cup (35g) cocoa powder in with the first batch of icing sugar.

To colour ready-made soft icing, start with a tiny drop of colouring and knead gently until colour is even before adding more colouring.

To colour butter cream, beat in a tiny drop of colouring thoroughly before adding more; it's easy to add too much, so use tiny amounts.

FLUFFY FROSTING

1 cup (220g) caster sugar
¹/₃ cup (80ml) water
2 egg whites

Combine sugar and the water in small saucepan; stir with a wooden spoon over high heat, without boiling, until sugar dissolves. Boil, uncovered, without stirring, about 3 to 5 minutes or until syrup is slightly thick. If a candy thermometer is available, the syrup will be ready when it reaches 114°C (240°F).

Otherwise, when the syrup is thick, remove the pan from the heat, allow the bubbles to subside then test the syrup by dropping 1 teaspoon into a cup of cold water. The syrup should form a ball of soft sticky toffee when rolled gently between your fingertips.

The syrup should not change colour; if it does, it has been cooked for too long and you will have to discard it and start again.

While syrup is boiling, beat egg whites in small bowl with electric mixer until stiff; keep beating (or whites will deflate) until syrup reaches the correct temperature.

When syrup is ready, allow bubbles to subside then pour a very thin stream onto the egg whites with mixer operating on medium speed. If syrup is added too quickly to the egg whites, frosting will not thicken. Continue beating and adding syrup until all syrup is used. Continue to beat until frosting stands in stiff peaks (frosting should be barely warm by this stage).

Tint frosting, if desired, by beating food colouring through while mixing, or by stirring through with spatula at the end. The flavour of the frosting can be varied by adding different flavoured extracts, such as almond, butterscotch, peppermint, lemon, etc.

For best results, frosting should be applied to a cake on the day it is to be served, while the frosting is still soft and has a marshmallow consistency. While you can frost the cake the day before, the frosting will become crisp and lose its glossy appearance, much like a meringue. Make sure to frost the cake around the base near the board; this forms a seal and helps keep the cake fresh.

PIPING GEL

Piping gel is sold in small tubes at supermarkets. If you prefer, make your own using the recipe below. Store the mixture in an airtight container in the refrigerator for up to a month; if it becomes too thick, stir in a tiny amount of water, a little at a time, until gel reaches a pipeable consistency.

¹/₃ cup (75g) caster sugar
1 tablespoon cornflour
¼ cup (60ml) lemon juice
¼ cup (60ml) water

Combine sugar and cornflour in small saucepan; gradually blend in juice then the water. Stir over high heat until mixture boils and thickens. Colour as desired.

It's important, when making fluffy frosting, to beat the mixture until it is almost cool.

A quick and easy piping bag can be made from baking paper – ideal for small amounts of icing.

EQUIPMENT

PIPING BAGS can be bought from cake-decorating or chefs' suppliers; these are usually made from a waterproof fabric, and can have screws attached to hold icing tubes. Alternatively, make bags from baking or greaseproof paper, which will hold various-shaped tubes. Cut the tips of the bags to the size required for piping. These are ideal for small amounts of icing or chocolate.

Another option is to use a small plastic bag. Push the icing (or chocolate) into the corner of the bag, twist the bag around the icing, then snip the tip to the desired size and shape.

Ready-made plastic piping bags can be bought from many supermarkets.

ICING TUBES are made from metal or plastic, and can be bought from cake-decorating suppliers, some craft shops, supermarkets and cookware shops.

NON-STICK ROLLING PINS are available from chefs' suppliers and cake-decorating suppliers as well as cookware shops. Candy thermometers, used to measure the temperature of syrups, are available from hardware and cookware shops. We used double-ended toothpicks throughout this book.

CANDY CAKE DECORATIONS made from sugar, corn starch and vegetable gum, are assorted lettering, pictures and shapes used for decorating cakes. These can easily be found at your local supermarket.

FOOD COLOURINGS

We used good-quality edible gels and concentrated pastes, which are available from cake-decorating suppliers and some health food stores. It's best to add minuscule amounts (using a skewer or toothpick) to the icing until the desired colour is reached. Use care when handling food colourings as they stain. Coloured icing can become darker or lighter on standing, so keep this in mind when decorating a cake ahead of time. If you have the time, it's a good idea to experiment by colouring a small amount of the icing, then covering or enclosing it with plastic wrap and allowing it to stand for a few hours to determine if the icing fades or darkens.

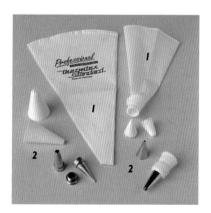

1 Piping bags 2 A variety of icing tubes, both plastic and metal

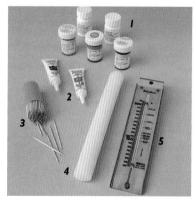

1 Food colouring 2 Decorating gel 3 Toothpicks 4 Non-stick rolling pin 5 Candy thermometer

DECORATIONS

Fruit Sticks

Musk Sticks

jelly beans

chocolate coins

large teeth lolly

sour apple karate belt

fruit Roll-Ups reel

white Life Savers

fruit Roll-Ups

Jelly Tots

snakes

chocolate car

chocolate fish

raspberry strap

small hearts

Five Flavours Life Savers

Brite Crawlers

Killer Python

small jelly snake

fruit rings

chocolate ladybird

large hearts

Fizzers

candy cane

jubes

Carnival Pop

spearmint leaves

Jaffa regular and giant

Screw Pop

orange segment jubes

black licorice rope

small lollipop

black licorice twist

Chunky Raspberry Twister

lollipop

red and green frogs

black licorice strap

red licorice rope

M&M's

Smarties

Kool Fruits

Kool Mints

Fruit Fantasy Strawberries

mini M&M's

small gum balls

Oompas

bananas

raspberries

gum balls

rainbow choc-chips

Crazy Bananas

milk bottles

cake decorating moon and stars

Skittles

blue boiled lollies

strawberries and creams

licorice allsorts

coloured sprinkles

Tic Tacs

jelly shark

hundreds & thousands allsorts

Bo-Peeps

round licorice allsorts

orange sprinkles

mini musks

yellow sprinkles

coloured cachous

silver and gold sugar-covered almonds

snowflakes

DECORATIONS

Sherbet cone

small ice-cream cone

potato straws

crinkle cut potato chips

waffle cone

Coco Pops

Mentos

Rice Bubbles

large round mints

pink ice-cream wafer

pink and white marshmallows

turkish delight

Mallow Bakes

large white marshmallow

pink fairy floss

coloured popcorn

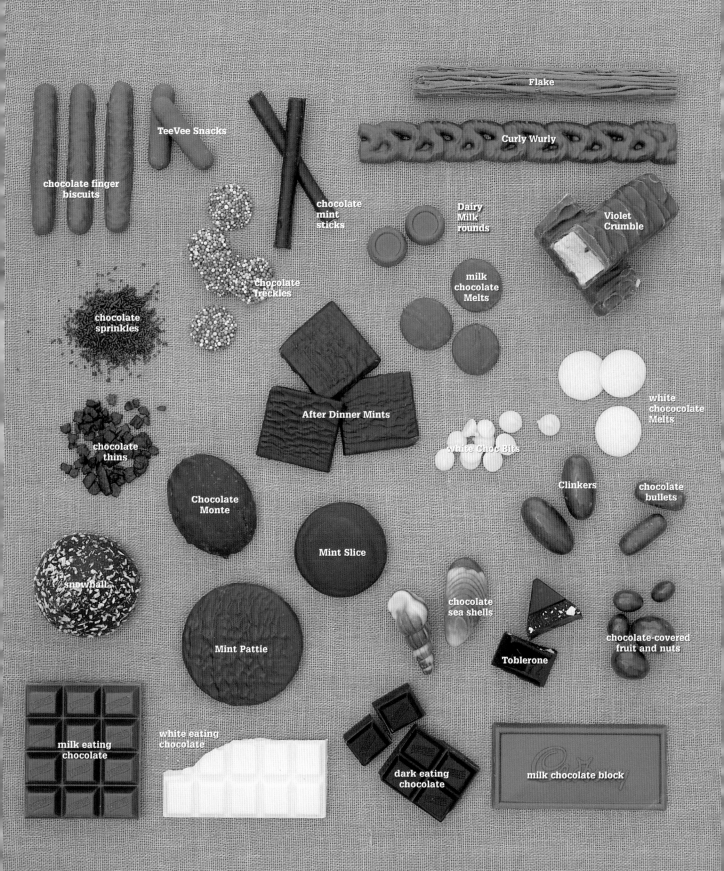

Flake

TeeVee Snacks

Curly Wurly

chocolate finger biscuits

chocolate mint sticks

Dairy Milk rounds

Violet Crumble

chocolate treckles

chocolate sprinkles

milk chocolate Melts

chocolate thins

After Dinner Mints

white chococolate Melts

white Choc Bits

Clinkers

chocolate bullets

Chocolate Monte

Mint Slice

snowball

chocolate sea shells

chocolate-covered fruit and nuts

Mint Pattie

Toblerone

milk eating chocolate

white eating chocolate

dark eating chocolate

milk chocolate block

GLOSSARY

baking paper also known as silicon paper, parchment or non-stick baking paper; not to be confused with greaseproof or waxed paper. Use it to line pans before cooking or baking and to make piping bags.

bicarbonate of soda also known as baking or carb soda.

butter use salted or unsalted (sweet) butter; 125g is equal to 1 stick (4 ounces) of butter.

cachous also called dragées in some countries; minuscule (3mm to 5mm) metallic-looking, but edible, confectionery balls used in cake decorating; available in silver, gold or various colours.

chenille sticks also known as pipe cleaners.

chocolate

choc Bits also known as chocolate chips or chocolate morsels; available in milk, white and dark chocolate.

dark eating also known as semi-sweet or luxury chocolate.

Melts small discs of compounded milk, white or dark chocolate; ideal for melting and moulding.

milk eating most popular eating chocolate; mild and very sweet.

white eating contains no cocoa solids but derives its sweet flavour from cocoa butter. Is very sensitive to heat.

cocoa powder also just called cocoa; unsweetened, dried, roasted then ground cocoa beans.

coconut

desiccated unsweetened, finely shredded, dried, concentrated coconut.

shredded thin strips of dried coconut flesh.

cornflour also known as cornstarch. Available made from corn or wheat.

cream

fresh also known as pure cream and pouring cream.

thickened a whipping cream containing a thickener.

cream of tartar the acid ingredient in baking powder; added to confectionery mixtures it helps prevent sugar crystallising. Keeps frostings creamy and improves volume when beating egg whites.

Dolly Varden pan spherical, bombe-shaped cake pan.

eggs we use large chicken eggs having an average weight of 60g.

flour

plain an all-purpose flour, made from wheat.

self-raising plain flour sifted with baking powder in the proportion of 1 cup plain flour to 2 teaspoons baking powder.

fried noodles crispy egg noodles that have been deep-fried then packaged for sale on supermarket shelves.

glossy decorating gel prepared icing available in different colours; comes in a tube with a small nozzle and used mainly to add outlines and other details.

ice-cream use good-quality ice-cream.

neapolitan vanilla, strawberry and chocolate ice-cream.

jam also known as conserve.

jam rolls large jam rollettes.

lamington pan 20cm x 30cm slab cake pan, 3cm deep.

light corn syrup an imported product available in some supermarkets, delicatessens and health food stores. Made from cornstarch, it is a popular ingredient in American cooking for frostings, jams and jellies.

milk we use full-cream milk unless otherwise stated in the recipe.

prunes commercially dried plums.

ready-made soft icing a prepared icing ready to roll or mould. Available from supermarkets.

savoiardi (sponge finger) biscuits also known as savoy biscuits or lady's fingers, they are Italian-style crisp fingers made from sponge cake mixture.

sugar

brown a soft, finely granulated sugar retaining molasses for its characteristic colour and flavour.

caster also known as superfine or finely granulated table sugar.

demerara small-grained golden-coloured crystal sugar.

icing sugar also known as confectioners' sugar or powdered sugar; granulated sugar crushed together with a small amount of cornflour.

pure icing sugar also known as confectioners' sugar or powdered sugar.

white we used coarse, granulated table sugar, also known as crystal sugar, unless otherwise specified.

sultanas seedless dried grapes; also known as golden raisins.

sweetened condensed milk a canned milk product consisting of milk with more than half the water content removed and sugar added to the remaining milk.

swiss roll pan also known as a jelly-roll pan. Measures 26cm x 32cm and has slightly raised sides.

vanilla

bean dried, long, thin pod from a tropical golden orchid; the tiny black seeds inside the bean are used to impart a luscious vanilla flavour in baking and desserts. A bean can be used three or four times before losing its flavour.

extract vanilla beans that have been submerged in alcohol. Vanilla essence is not a suitable substitute.

vegetable oil any number of oils, sourced from plants rather than animal fats.

CONVERSION CHART

Wherever you live, you'll be able to use our recipes with the help of these easy-to-follow conversions. While these conversions are approximate only, the difference between an exact and the approximate conversion of various liquid and dry measures is minimal and will not affect your cooking results.

DRY MEASURES

METRIC	IMPERIAL
15g	½oz
30g	1oz
60g	2oz
90g	3oz
125g	4oz (¼lb)
155g	5oz
185g	6oz
220g	7oz
250g	8oz (½lb)
280g	9oz
315g	10oz
345g	11oz
375g	12oz (¾lb)
410g	13oz
440g	14oz
470g	15oz
500g	16oz (1lb)
750g	24oz (1½lb)
1kg	32oz (2lb)

LIQUID MEASURES

METRIC	IMPERIAL
30ml	1 fluid oz
60ml	2 fluid oz
100ml	3 fluid oz
125ml	4 fluid oz
150ml	5 fluid oz (¼ pint/1 gill)
190ml	6 fluid oz
250ml	8 fluid oz
300ml	10 fluid oz (½ pint)
500ml	16 fluid oz
600ml	20 fluid oz (1 pint)
1000ml (1 litre)	1¾ pints

HELPFUL MEASURES

METRIC	IMPERIAL
3mm	⅛in
6mm	¼in
1cm	½in
2cm	¾in
2.5cm	1in
5cm	2in
6cm	2½in
8cm	3in
10cm	4in
13cm	5in
15cm	6in
18cm	7in
20cm	8in
23cm	9in
25cm	10in
28cm	11in
30cm	12in (1ft)

MEASURING EQUIPMENT

The difference between one country's measuring cups and another's is, at most, within a 2 or 3 teaspoon variance. (For the record, one Australian metric measuring cup holds approximately 250ml.) The most accurate way of measuring dry ingredients is to weigh them. When measuring liquids, use a clear glass or plastic jug with the metric markings. (One Australian metric tablespoon holds 20ml; one Australian metric teaspoon holds 5ml.)

HOW TO MEASURE

When using graduated metric measuring cups, shake dry ingredients loosely into the appropriate cup. Do not tap the cup on a bench or tightly pack the ingredients unless directed to do so. Level top of measuring cups and measuring spoons with a knife. When measuring liquids, place a clear glass or plastic jug with metric markings on a flat surface to check accuracy at eye level.

Note: North America, NZ and the UK use 15ml tablespoons. All cup and spoon measurements are level.

We use large eggs having an average weight of 60g.

OVEN TEMPERATURES

These oven temperatures are only a guide. Always check the manufacturer's manual.

	°C (CELSIUS)	°F (FAHRENHEIT)	GAS MARK
Very slow	120	250	½
Slow	150	275-300	1-2
Moderately slow	160	325	3
Moderate	180	350-375	4-5
Moderately hot	200	400	6
Hot	220	425-450	7-8
Very hot	240	475	9

INDEX

ARE YOU MISSING SOME COOKBOOKS?

The Australian Women's Weekly Cookbooks are available from bookshops, cookshops, supermarkets and other stores all over the world. You can also buy direct from the publisher, using the order form below.

TITLE	RRP	QTY	TITLE	RRP	QTY
100 Fast Fillets	£6.99		Grills	£6.99	
A Taste of Chocolate	£6.99		Healthy Heart Cookbook	£6.99	
After Work Fast	£6.99		Indian Cooking Class	£6.99	
Beginners Cooking Class	£6.99		Japanese Cooking Class	£6.99	
Beginners Thai	£6.99		Just For One	£6.99	
Best Food Fast	£6.99		Just For Two	£6.99	
Breads & Muffins	£6.99		Kids' Birthday Cakes	£6.99	
Brunches, Lunches & Treats	£6.99		Kids Cooking	£6.99	
Cafe Classics	£6.99		Kids' Cooking Step-by-Step	£6.99	
Cafe Favourites	£6.99		Low-carb, Low-fat	£6.99	
Cakes Bakes & Desserts	£6.99		Low-fat Food for Life	£6.99	
Cakes Biscuits & Slices	£6.99		Low-fat Meals in Minutes	£6.99	
Cakes Cooking Class	£6.99		Main Course Salads	£6.99	
Caribbean Cooking	£6.99		Mexican	£6.99	
Casseroles	£6.99		Middle Eastern Cooking Class	£6.99	
Casseroles & Slow-Cooked Classics	£6.99		Mince in Minutes	£6.99	
Cheap Eats	£6.99		Moroccan & the Foods of North Africa	£6.99	
Cheesecakes: baked and chilled	£6.99		Muffins, Scones & Breads	£6.99	
Chicken	£6.99		New Casseroles	£6.99	
Chicken Meals in Minutes	£6.99		New Curries	£6.99	
Chinese and the foods of Thailand, Vietnam, Malaysia & Japan	£6.99		New Finger Food	£6.99	
			New French Food	£6.99	
Chinese Cooking Class	£6.99		New Salads	£6.99	
Christmas Cooking	£6.99		Party Food and Drink	£6.99	
Chocs & Treats	£6.99		Pasta Meals in Minutes	£6.99	
Cocktails	£6.99		Potatoes	£6.99	
Cookies & Biscuits	£6.99		Quick & Simple Cooking	£6.99	
Cooking Class Cake Decorating	£6.99		Rice & Risotto	£6.99	
Cupcakes & Fairycakes	£6.99		Sauces Salsas & Dressings	£6.99	
Detox	£6.99		Sensational Stir-Fries	£6.99	
Dinner Lamb	£6.99		Simple Healthy Meals	£6.99	
Easy Comfort Food	£6.99		Simple Starters Mains & Puds	£6.99	
Easy Curry	£6.99		Soup	£6.99	
Easy Midweek Meals	£6.99		Stir-fry	£6.99	
Easy Spanish-Style	£6.99		Superfoods for Exam Success	£6.99	
Food for Fit and Healthy Kids	£6.99		Tapas Mezze Antipasto & other bites	£6.99	
Foods of the Mediterranean	£6.99		Thai Cooking Class	£6.99	
Foods That Fight Back	£6.99		Traditional Italian	£6.99	
Fresh Food Fast	£6.99		Vegetarian Meals in Minutes	£6.99	
Fresh Food for Babies & Toddlers	£6.99		Vegie Food	£6.99	
Good Food for Babies & Toddlers	£6.99		Wicked Sweet Indulgences	£6.99	
Great Kids' Cakes (May 08)	£6.99		Wok Meals in Minutes	£6.99	
Greek Cooking Class	£6.99		TOTAL COST:	£	

Mr/Mrs/Ms _____

Address_____ Postcode_____

Day time phone _____ email* (optional)_____

I enclose my cheque/money order for £ _____

or please charge £ _____

to my: ☐ Access ☐ Mastercard ☐ Visa ☐ Diners Club

Card number ☐☐☐☐ ☐☐☐☐ ☐☐☐☐ ☐☐☐☐

Expiry date _____ 3 digit security code *(found on reverse of card)* _____

Cardholder's name_____ Signature _____

To order: Mail or fax – photocopy or complete the order form above, and send your credit card details or cheque payable to: Australian Consolidated Press (UK), ACP Books, 10 Scirocco Close, Moulton Park Office Village, Northampton NN3 6AP. phone (+44) (0)1604 642200 fax (+44) (0)1604 642300 email books@acpuk.com or order online at www.acpuk.com **Non-UK residents:** We accept the credit cards listed on the coupon, or cheques, drafts or International Money Orders payable in sterling and drawn on a UK bank. Credit card charges are at the exchange rate current at the time of payment. **Postage and packing UK:** Add £1.00 per order plus £1.75 per book. **Postage and packing overseas:** Add £2.00 per order plus £3.50 per book. All pricing current at time of going to press and subject to change/availability. **Offer ends 31.12.2008**

* By including your email address, you consent to receipt of any email regarding this magazine, and other emails which inform you of ACP's other publications, products, services and events, and to promote third party goods and services you may be interested in.

TEST KITCHEN
Food director Pamela Clark
Associate food editor Alexandra Somerville
Home economists Emma Braz, Kimberley Coverdale, Nadia French, Amanda Kelly, Sarah O'Brien, Maria Sampsonis
Photographers Robert Clark, Robert Taylor
Stylists Carolyn Fienberg, Jane Hann, Cherise Koch, Sophia Young

ACP BOOKS
General manager Christine Whiston
Editorial director Susan Tomnay
Creative director Hieu Chi Nguyen
Designer Hannah Blackmore
Senior editor Wendy Bryant
Director of sales Brian Cearnes
Marketing manager Bridget Cody
Business analyst Ashley Davies
Operations manager David Scotto
International rights enquires Laura Bamford
lbamford@acpuk.com

ACP Books are published by ACP Magazines a division of PBL Media Pty Limited
Group publisher, Women's lifestyle Pat Ingram
Director of sales, Women's lifestyle Lynette Phillips
Commercial manager, Women's lifestyle Seymour Cohen
Marketing director, Women's lifestyle Matthew Dominello
Public relations manager, Women's lifestyle Hannah Deveraux
Creative director, Events, Women's lifestyle Luke Bonnano
Research Director, Women's lifestyle Justin Stone
ACP Magazines, Chief Executive officer Scott Lorson
PBL Media, Chief Executive officer Ian Law
Produced by ACP Books, Sydney.
Printed by Dai Nippon Printing in Korea.
Published by ACP Books, a division of ACP Magazines Ltd, 54 Park St, Sydney; GPO Box 4088, Sydney, NSW 2001.
Ph: (02) 9282 8618 Fax: (02) 9267 9438.
acpbooks@acpmagazines.com.au
www.acpbooks.com.au
To order books, phone 136 116 (within Australia).
Send recipe enquiries to:
recipeenquiries@acpmagazines.com.au
Australia Distributed by Network Services, phone +61 2 9282 8777 fax +61 2 9264 3278 networkweb@networkservicescompany.com.au
United Kingdom Distributed by Australian Consolidated Press (UK), phone (01604) 642 200 fax (01604) 642 300 books@acpuk.com
Canada Distributed by Publishers Group Canada phone (800) 663 5714 fax (800) 565 3770 service@raincoast.com
New Zealand Distributed by Netlink Distribution Company, phone (9) 366 9966 ask@ndc.co.nz
South Africa Distributed by PSD Promotions, phone (27 11) 392 6065/7 fax (27 11) 392 6079/80 orders@psdprom.co.za

A catalogue record for this book is available from the British Library. Includes index.
ISBN 978-1-86396-729-7.
© ACP Magazines Ltd 2008
ABN 18 053 273 546